Raise Your Frequency,
Transform Your Life

"*Raise Your Frequency, Transform Your Life* is not just a book; it's a transformative journey that redefines our perception of life's challenges. This channeled masterpiece offers profound insights into turning everyday struggles into stepping stones for spiritual growth. With a compassionate and loving approach, Selina Maitreya guides us to elevate our internal frequency, showing that the true pathway to a deeper spiritual life lies in embracing and responding to life's daily difficulties with love. A must-read for anyone on the path of self-discovery and spiritual awakening."

JEFFREY VAN DYK,
FOUNDER OF THE COURAGEOUS MESSENGER

"In compassionate, accessible, and remarkably relatable terms, Maitreya shares her personal odyssey with life's curveballs and sagaciously demonstrates how we can rise above conflicts to unlock our highest spiritual potential. Drawing from her most challenging life experiences, she provides real-life applications that transform difficulties into tools for personal growth, guiding us on a journey to create an extraordinary life."

LESLIE HOFFMAN,
FOUNDER AND CEO OF HOFFMAN GROUP

"I have read hundreds of books on abundance, spirituality, and awareness and *Raise Your Frequency, Transform Your Life* is one of the best. In a very down-to-earth style, Selina Maitreya shares insights that will be enjoyed by those new to their spiritual journey as well as those who have been on their path for decades. Readers are taken into the private world of Selina's own journey, allowing for a connection with her on a very deep level. The processes she shares throughout the book allow for hands-on experience of shifting one's relationship to oneself. This book will be a great addition to any seeker's personal growth library."

KATHLEEN GAGE, FOUNDER OF VEGAN VISIBILITY, KEYNOTE SPEAKER, AND BUSINESS CONSULTANT

"We live in a fast-paced world filled with so many disappointments and challenges. Selina Maitreya has written a book that offers a light and guides us through the chaos of our modern world. She takes us through powerful exercises to help us live the life we want and be able to truly release our never-ending anxiety, providing actual, practical, transformative tools that will take us to inner peace. A powerful spiritual leader, Selina takes her decades of experience and now offers it to us through this book that is a warm and deep hug of love."

NIKÓL ROGERS, EMPOWERMENT COACH AND CREATOR OF THE ZENRED METHOD

Raise Your Frequency, Transform Your Life

*How to Respond with Love
to Life's Difficulties*

Selina Maitreya

Destiny Books
Rochester, Vermont

Destiny Books
One Park Street
Rochester, Vermont 05767
www.Destiny Books.com

Destiny Books is a division of Inner Traditions International

Cataloging-in-Publication Data for this title is available from the Library of Congress

ISBN 979-8-88850-046-0 (print)
ISBN 979-8-88850-047-7 (ebook)

Printed and bound in the United States by Lake Book Manufacturing, LLC

10 9 8 7 6 5 4 3 2 1

Text design and layout by Kenleigh Manseau
This book was typeset in Garamond Premier Pro

To send correspondence to the author of this book, mail a first-class letter to the author c/o Inner Traditions • Bear & Company, One Park Street, Rochester, VT 05767, and we will forward the communication, or contact the author directly at **practicalspiritualitywithselina.com** or **selina@selinamaitreya.com**.

Scan the QR code and save 25% at InnerTraditions.com. Browse over 2,000 titles on spirituality, the occult, ancient mysteries, new science, holistic health, and natural medicine.

This book would never have been written if the Reverend Janice "Hope" Gorman had not come into my life as my teacher.

Hope's brilliance, humility, and kindness, as well as her humor and her unfailing warmth and generosity, are experienced by all who have the good fortune to be in her presence.

May you shine on brightly for many years to come, Beloved!

☾

I was introduced to Reverend Janice "Hope" Gorman over twenty-five years ago, and to this day she has continually guided my spiritual journey by sharing information from the masters that I continually take into my life. Spirit started channeling through me during one of my first sessions with Hope. Her guidance as to what was needed in order to continue to be a clear channel was incredibly helpful to me, as a young chela, and is followed to this very day.

During 2018, still healing an extensive brain injury, I went through a tough spot as I wrote this book. I needed some clarity and asked Hope if I could visit the Hope Interfaith Center (HIC) for a week. She surprised me with her response: "Why not come for six months and be our first teacher in residence?" she asked. I excitedly accepted her invitation and lived at the center, during which time much of this book was written.

It is no exaggeration to say that living at the center for an extended period of time provided me the most incredibly perfect location for writing a book directed by Spirit. The frequency at HIC is one of inclusiveness and high vibration, and living in that space informed and energized every word I wrote. I am so grateful to my teacher, Hope, for everything she has brought and continues to bring to me and to the world, and I dedicate this book to her.

Contents

Origin Story

Every book written has its own birth story, and this book's creation has been deeply interconnected with my life's spiritual and physical journey for the past ten years. Writing this book has taken me on an odyssey in the physical world that totally intersects with the purpose of the material. As I wrote, I knew Spirit was talking to me as much as Spirit was sharing the information for you.

The book you are about to read contains information that seeks to inform you about the truth and purpose of difficulty in your life. It offers practical spiritual exercises that you can use to transform any tragedies, daily irritations, or stresses into tools for conscious transformation that will bring you peace.

How perfect for the masters of Oneness, then, to ask me to channel their wisdom and write this book during a time when my brain was severely injured, a time when I faced my most difficult physical challenges. And yet it was also a time where my connection to Source was full and complete—more active than it had ever been in my life.

The book began in 2013 when I lived in New York City. I had just sold my home of twenty years in New England—the place where, as a single parent, I had raised my two boys. I had bettered the predictions of my friends and family who told me when I got divorced fifteen years earlier that I'd never be able to keep our house and that

I'd end up living in poverty. But due to my deep spiritual work and lots of physical world effort, I successfully kept my boys in their home, made a wonderful life for us all, and put them both through college with the help of their dad. Now, here I was: our house was sold, my boys were well into their new lives, and I was off to New York City ready to leave my consulting career behind and embrace being a spiritual teacher full time.

Everything was going to plan until two days before the closing on our house. With all my belongings packed up, the house was empty, and it was the first day of the rest of my life. On a gorgeous, sunny summer day, I was so excited as I drove from a local motel to clean the house for the last time. I came to a red light, and when it turned green, I moved into the intersection just as a woman ran a red light and hit my sports car at 70 mph, smack into the driver's door.

After a most mystical experience in the car, I was pulled out with the jaws of life and ultimately diagnosed with an intense, traumatic brain injury that left me alive but unable to function well and live anything close to a normal life.

Spirit directed me to move forward with my existing plans, and I moved to New York City. But being with people was impossible because every sound was a dagger in my brain, and I couldn't hold a conversation for more than a few minutes without tremendous effort. I was completely physically exhausted twenty-four hours a day. Taking a shower was a victory. And while I was in the greatest city in the world, I couldn't go to a restaurant, movie, museum, or a play without great difficulty. My physical and intellectual disabilities were huge and went on for the next four years.

However, magically during this time I had a connection and entree to Oneness that I had never experienced before. I would simply close my eyes and be in a paradigm where everything was more than easy. There was no physical pain, no sensation, no noise, and nothing to see, for there was simply nothing.

I was nothing.

I floated in this field of Oneness many hours every day, because in Oneness was the respite that I had always sought, and all I had to do was close my eyes and breathe.

This exquisite invitation began in the car when I was knocked out on impact. The car immediately filled with a profound light, and Spirit told me then that this was an event that had been orchestrated. I was informed that I'd be taken out of my life but not taken out of the world. I was told to completely surrender, and Spirit would take care of the daily details. I was advised that my energetic systems would be completely reorganized and my greatest wish, to be a spiritual teacher and a guide, would be delivered unto me.

What I wasn't told then was that soon a request would be made of me that would seem almost impossible to fulfill.

I had been channeling the energy of Oneness for more than ten years. I was deeply comfortable parking my personality and ego, making space for the energy of the Divine to speak through me to others. But it was a huge surprise when Spirit came through and told me that I was to be the steward of a book that would help people learn how to use difficulty as a transformational tool to increase their consciousness and experience peace. What I was to write about was exactly what I was living!

The problem was I couldn't even type. I had no memory, and my normal organizational skills were completely gone.

But I have always said yes to Spirit regardless of how illogical and seemingly impossible the requests were. I had no idea how I could facilitate the commitment I had made, but I knew if Spirit wanted this book to find its way into the world, we would accomplish that!

Thus began a six-year journey to write the book that you are holding in your hands.

Messages came through daily, and I recorded them on my phone for the next four years. During this time, Spirit shared what you are about to read—teachings and practices that empower you to respond to daily chaos from love.

While the material was mesmerizing and powerful, my daily life was extremely difficult. Yet I was committed to not allowing my difficulty to impede my progress with the book. I heeded the advice that Spirit was channeling through me to live beyond my circumstances, and I continued on.

During the writing and early brain healing period, my life had been completely upended by my injury. I had let go of a relationship with a man that I loved because I just didn't have enough energy to move through my daily life, write the book, and still be able to contribute to a committed relationship. My financial status had changed dramatically, and I went from a more than comfortable life to claiming bankruptcy and living off every penny that I earned.

Once my brain was healed enough for me to be able to use my computer more efficiently, I began the task of transcribing the words of Spirit into a manuscript. During that time, I was directed to move once again, this time out of New York City, and I was brought most gratefully to the woods of Woodstock, New York. I quickly met my editor Nancy Butler-Ross, and with her help I was able to structure and organize the volume of sacred material into a book.

It is not lost on me, Beloved, how I was able to supersede my brain injury and painstakingly, word by word, page by page, craft a book that I knew would be life changing for so many. As I responded to my own difficulty from love and lived beyond my circumstances, I was experiencing a sense of peace that I had never felt before.

It was also not surprising that Spirit saw to move me two more times, with each move providing exactly what my healing and the book needed. My brain was deeply wounded, and I know it was my connection to Spirit that enabled me to perform the skills that were needed to write the book. Six years later the book was complete, and the process of bringing it to market began.

I was called to put my energy, time, and money into marketing the book to publishers and agents. I had only a few hours each week for book efforts over the time allotted to earn a living, and two years later, after receiving no positive response, I began to feel defeated. In a conversation with Spirit, I was reminded of the book's contents and my commitment to my work of responding to chaos from love. I was told to lie the book down, stop marketing it, and allow Spirit to set the timeline for publication. Spirit advised me to create a work-study program around the book and to share the information with my current spiritual students. I followed this guidance and ended up taking three groups of students through a ten-month course using the material in this book.

It was outstanding and overwhelming to see the changes that the students made in their lives as they used the material, for each time they responded to difficulty from love, they raised their frequency and transformed their lives.

Out of the blue, in late 2022, one of the people I had met during my time in New York offered to make an introduction of the material to Inner Traditions • Bear & Company. I consulted Spirit as to whether I should take up this invitation, and Spirit responded YES!

The introduction led to a conversation with Jon, Inner Traditions' acquisitions editor, and speaking with him felt like a conversation with an old friend.

Within a few days, they chose to publish the book.

I share this information with you now, dear reader, as I want you to know how magical and perfect the birth journey of this book has been.

I also want you to hear that the author of this book has been on her own journey of discovery—learning how to respond to difficulty from love—and the writing of this book was just that, for me.

This is a book that teaches you how to use any type of difficulty in your life as an opportunity for you to increase your consciousness, raise your vibration, and transform your life.

At a time in my life where I should have been off onto my new greatest adventure post motherhood, all of my plans stopped in the blink of an eye. What I knew then and know now is that my connection to Source, as well as my willingness to supersede my current physical chaos and respond to each piece of difficulty from love, truly enabled me to move forward to heal and write the book that you are about to dive into.

Today I am back in Massachusetts living close to family and friends. My brain is 90 percent healed, and I work a five-hour workday. I teach daily and live on a beautiful pond surrounded by nature as I rebuild my financial and personal life.

It is here that you find me, grateful to deliver to you the creation of my commitment to Spirit so many years ago, for the material you are holding in your hands contains the wisdom that brought me back into the world. Not surprisingly, much of the information that I was given and that I used to rebuild my world, you will find within the pages of this book. The material shared here will empower you to respond to any difficulty and every tragedy from a new, higher vibration, which will raise your frequency and transform your life.

That is my promise to you.

Acknowledgments

Every human journey provides us with the opportunity to be loved and supported as we find our way to our truth and to our purpose. I have been so blessed by the many relationships gifted to me: wise teachers to guide me to the light, friends who become family, and family that know, love, and accept all of who I am.

My endless gratitude to my guides: The masters of Oneness (aka Spirit), Reverend Janice "Hope" Gorman, Barbara Chanthra Prince, and Pamela Cucinell. The many years that I have been blessed by your presence have provided the wisdom and the way and have seeded the information provided in this book.

My family is small yet powerful.

I am forever grateful for my son Jake, for his ever-present, unwavering love and support, and I say prayers of thanks daily for my daughter-in-law Ali, who is a beacon of love and light.

I am grateful for my son Sam, his wife, T.J., and their family, who continue to provide me with love and opportunities to grow my consciousness.

I am gifted with the love of my sons' dad Ed, my brother Robert, my cousins Carol, Dave, and Wendy, my niece Amanda and her family, as well as Laura Stone, Wayne Martin, and their crew.

There are simply no words that can thank Leslie Jean-Bart enough for his love, support, and kindness to me during the early years of my brain injury and the writing of this book.

The power of women is perhaps one of life's greatest gifts, and my tribe of superb women has supported and loved me for years. I treasure them and am indebted to Sage Peterson, Paula Duva, Laura Stone, Jenny Gulliver, Jane Ceraso, Andy Migner, Laura Bonicelli, Priscilla Shute, and Audrey Mosely.

To all of my students past and present, thank you. Thank you for your commitment to the work, and for helping our planet to evolve, for each shift you have made on your journey has shifted us all. I am honored to have played a part in your awakening and it's been a true pleasure to witness each one of you, choosing to accept your job of creating the peace that you seek.

To my beloved Monks Without Monasteries group members: Sage Peterson, Diana Morales, Milijana Drobnjak, Deborah Hinkley, Gail Spriggs, Sue Renard, Susan Silverman, Ivy Greenberg, David Monroe, Julia Simkin, and Julia Zave: thank you seems hardly enough.

Each month as we focused on a different chapter from the book, you used the truths and practices shared to shift your world. Your efforts have contributed not only to the amazing changes you are now personally witnessing in your life, but I truly believe that each meeting we had and each effort you have made to transform difficulty into grace has helped to birth the book into the physical world.

My thanks to Linda Lowen for early editorial guidance and support, to Jan Goldstoff for the introduction to Inner Traditions, and to my assistant Melanie Borowczyk, who has kept the back end of my teaching business growing and going for many years. Thank you, Melanie, for your never-ending patience and kindness.

The job of an editor is a thankless one, and my undying gratitude goes to Nancy Butler-Ross. Nancy worked beside me to edit the original manuscript and supported me so kindly as I sought to take the book to market. Her consistent belief in the importance of the material and the book's need to be in the world was the juice I needed at times to carry on.

My gratitude is also extended to the continually patient and always knowledgeable team at Inner Traditions. From my first conversation with Jon Graham to my work with the editorial board and with

Kelly Bowen, Manzanita Carpenter Sanz, Erica Robinson, Ashley Kolesnik, Mercedes E. Rojas, and Jamaica Burns Griffin, the experience has been consistently supportive and energizing.

Finally, I thank Diana Martin "Chica," the Mighty Chuck Morrison, and the Giebitz clan—Rob, Bill, and Marcy—who oh so long ago introduced me to the world of Spirit for the very first time. You invited a fifteen-year-old girl who was lonely and suffering into your hearts and into a circle of friends that became a lifeline for me. The introduction to the world of magic, ritual, spirits, and consciousness that you shared became my life's journey.

Welcome to the First Day of the Rest of Your Life!

Y ou are reading these words as you are at an important juncture in your life, a spot that even you may not have recognized.

You are ready to utilize all your experiences of stress, pain, and even life tragedies as transformational tools that enable you to create an extraordinary life, one where you live in high vibration and experience peace and abundance regardless of what is transpiring in your physical world.

That's why this book is in your hands.

Before you wonder if you have read correctly or if I am crazy, be advised this is no ordinary spiritual or self-help book, and yes, responding to difficulty of any stripe from the frequency of love is an action that raises your personal vibration and takes you to peace.

As my Grandma Lilly would say, "Who knew?"

The material you are about to read has been channeled from the master consciousness known as Oneness. While no other book has approached in this way the opportunity to use life's difficulties as tools for raising one's awareness and building an abundant life, my students and I have practiced and lived this guidance for years. We are walking proof that what you are about to read truly works. Our results of responding to life's challenges from the highest frequency of love has continually delivered daily experiences that are both subtle and extraordinary.

It is my promise to you that as you sit in the energy of the teachings within this book and continually utilize the practices in your daily life as a response to the chaos and pain you experience, you, too, will raise your frequency and transform your life.

This is a spiritually directed practical book filled with truths and experiential action steps as well as stories from my students who have been using this information repeatedly. Within these pages you will find a road map to follow, but the journey is yours to take as you learn how to use daily chaos as the vehicle that will move you from pain to peace.

As you take on the work of using the difficulty that lands in your world as a tool to transform into grace, you will be creating a new lifestyle that is based on pivotal spiritual concepts, including:

- You are not a one-dimensional being—a "me" or an "I." You are indeed a multidimensional being: a physical form that contains a brain, a developed personality, an emotional body, a low field of energy (ego) that contains your history of pain, and your intuitive body, a high-frequency field that is your true north.
- Your intuitive body is your soul level, the field of Oneness, the energy of love that came into your body to have a physical experience. This is the aspect of your being that is meant to be your daily response to life's challenges, yet now is most likely lying dormant within you, waiting to be activated.
- Your conditioned belief that your physical brain and emotional body are the only tools you have to use when making choices in your life is what has led to much of the pain you may now experience. It is also what has kept you from the opportunity to raise your frequency and transform your life.
- Your choice of response to daily stress, difficulty, and even tragedy is paradoxically the most important and available tool you have to experience gratitude, peace, and understanding.
- Every bit of physical world difficulty has a higher-octave purpose— a purpose that focuses on the soul of you rather than the egoic

nature of you—and when you choose to activate your intuitive body, responding to chaos from love, you are using difficulty exactly as it was meant to be utilized.

- Using all of your daily life experiences as your practice pad and responding from love when challenges arise increases your consciousness and, over time, enables you to walk in the energy of equanimity, which raises your personal vibration and prepares the foundation for you to become the abundant being you were always meant to be.

In this book you will learn how to recognize your current state and then begin to respond to any chaos or fear (low energy) from your intuitive body (high frequency) that shows up as patience, kindness, understanding, tolerance, and gratitude.

By shifting in the moment of response out of the low energy and into the new higher field, you are raising your frequency!

Done consistently, every difficult moment you experience will be transformed into a moment of abundance, and your personal vibration will continue to rise. As your personal frequency increases you will begin to attract the people, situations, and events that will represent your individual wishes and desires.

Can you see now that when you choose to respond to difficulty from love, you are shifting the energetic dynamic around you and enabling new positive possibilities to arise?

In this book you will find teachings that I'm sure will make you stop and question your previous definition of what an extraordinary life truly looks like for you.

You will have an opportunity to see where you are now and be able to take a deep dive into where and when you are able to live inside the energy of positive response to life—and when you are not.

I'll share with you the most common blocks to leading an extraordinary life that most people hold, and I'll provide you with action steps for each one that you can take, *now*, in order to move through any barriers that may currently be in place.

Throughout, I share stories from my own and my students' lives that will inspire you and remind you that we all can create equanimity and peace no matter where we are on our path or how challenging our life circumstances are!

Most importantly, as you use the actions I provide, you will be shifting into high frequency and you will see your life resonate at an entirely different level. How can it not? For you are an energetic being, and as you choose to respond to any irritation, difficulty, or tragedy from a state of grace and peace, you are creating your next moment from a higher vibration.

The book you are holding is meant to be a workbook. Yes, you can read through the entire text, highlighting words and phrases that hold meaning for you as you go along, but then do go back and *do the work that is offered.*

In between the completion of this book and its publication, I created small groups where I took students through a ten-month work-study program. Each month I would introduce a different chapter of this book. I shared a channeled teaching and reviewed the exercises that were created for the information in that chapter. Group members then went back into their lives and read the material and noticed during the month where their life presented them opportunities to use the practices in the current chapter. They did the work needed and noticed their energy shifting, which brought about entirely different results than they had ever experienced before. We'd come back after four weeks and everyone would share what happened in their life—where the work showed up, what they did with it, how their frequency had been raised, and finally, how through using the practices offered they were able to rise above each challenging experience and feel true peace.

It became evident to me then, as it still is now, that Spirit has given me this book to give to you so you can use the information in your daily life as you move forward. That's why I'm inviting you to take your time with each chapter: read the material, look at the practices offered, and then keep the information and exercises in your awareness so you can use them as called for as you move through the days ahead. When you feel ready to move forward to the next chapter, do so and approach the rest of the book in a similar way.

This is a book that will become your daily guide. You'll be able to pick it up at any time and have different sections speak to where your life is in that very moment. Whether you are experiencing procrastination or you've just received a dire health diagnosis, this book is the vehicle that will empower and teach you how to use your difficulty as a transformational tool to bring you to peace.

Using the information and practices supplied, over time your life will become an expression of your conscious efforts, and you will feel a deep sense of gratitude and calm regardless of whatever chaos lands in your world. In this energetic space you will be able to manifest the wishes and hopes you truly desire into the physical world with more ease. This, my friend, is when you will recognize that you are using your challenging daily experiences as tools to raise your frequency and transform your life!

In case you're wondering, I've written this book for a general audience, not only for readers already attuned to spiritual work. *Everyone* experiences difficulty, yet few people have the knowledge that chaotic times are meant to be used as a tool to take you to higher consciousness, and fewer know how to actually shift their frequency in the moment of emotional stress.

If you're new to spiritual thinking, the practical intentions, teachings, tools, and exercises I share will be highly accessible, profoundly revelatory, and totally transformational. If you are already comfortable as a spiritual seeker, the book will offer you the empirical tools that will empower you to finally integrate your spiritual beliefs into your daily life. As you embody your holy values you will become the spiritually directed being that you have always aspired to be.

In my role as spiritual mentor, I have become a teacher of teachers sharing these concepts and practices throughout the world with business leaders, wellness professionals, and holistic guides. I have been continually excited to see how my students' lives have quickly changed in the most remarkable ways, as they have used the teachings and practices that I am honored to share here and now with you.

Let's begin!

1

Your Extraordinary Life Awaits

Transformational Goal: *Reactivate Your Frequency of Love*

As we begin, Spirit shares a different version than you might hold of your early years and their purpose in regards to understanding the work ahead. Spirit explains the use of free will and introduces to you the concept of societal conditioning and your choice to move beyond any prior acceptance of information that no longer serves you. Finally, Spirit offers you a totally new purpose for the difficulty you experience in your life. As you see the totality of who you truly are, you are introduced to your energy fields—the major tools for transformation that you will use to create a new response to all of the difficulty you experience in order to raise your frequency and transform your life!

Your History: A Recap

You were born seeded with the high-frequency energy of your creator that I refer to as love, as Oneness, as higher consciousness, *as your intuitive body.* This vibration is the purest form of abundance, and it was activated in physical form with your first breath.

At that moment all you knew was love, and in that frequency anything was possible, as Oneness was your totality. You had no history of pain in your body, as your personality and history had yet to develop.

The moment you took your first breath was perhaps also the last time you totally experienced the full abundance that is your natural inheritance. For as you came into the physical world, a whole new paradigm of existence awaited you, one that was the antithesis of the divinity of which you are an expression.

In addition to being endowed with the vibration of love, you were also given the gift of free will. In its purest sense, free will can be simply defined as the ability to say no to the high frequency of love that was gifted to you.

This is where your life began, with all possibilities in front of you and the opportunity to say no to any or all of them. Paradox in its truest form, you were and are an expression of divinity and the physicality of the planet you were birthed upon.

A result of this paradoxical reality, you had the opportunity to choose your state in each and every moment as you moved from being an infant to child to adult. This choice was unknown to you then and still may be undiscovered, yet it is your greatest freedom.

It is also what has kept you from manifesting an extraordinary life.

As exchanges and events happened in your life, as chaos appeared, you had the opportunity to choose your response in each moment. Your personal frequency shifted as a reflection of your choices. When you chose a loving reply to the chaos that appeared, you created your next moment from that energy. When you chose to leave your highest wisdom behind, and you responded from your lower frequencies of anger, jealousy, and frustration, you moved farther and farther from your light and created experiences that reflected the chaos you were buried inside of.

Your life up to now, and your experience of peace or lack of it, is the result of all of your choices.

Had you known from an early age that your life is directed by the frequency of the responses you choose, and had you had the tools to do so, you most certainly would have chosen a positive response to each and every piece of difficulty that landed in your lap. However, this information was not available to you. It was most likely not how your caretakers lived their lives, and certainly not what was delivered to you by your society.

Here is my gift to you: *You were meant to live a life of abundance and peace. This is what I call an extraordinary life.* The lack of this one critical piece of knowledge has led to years of unconscious behavior that has taken you away from the light that lives within you and from the rewarding life you were meant to live. Please read that again. *You were meant to live a life of abundance and peace.*

During your lifetime, not knowing that you had this type of choice of response to the difficulties that arose and not being aware that your choices always add up to the vibration of abundance you are able to experience, you often responded from the same frequency of what was delivered to you.

When you experienced kindness, you responded in kind, and when you experienced difficulty you were difficult back, which closed the door to your highest wisdom. You had no way of knowing that chaos can be answered with love. You never knew that difficulty is a part of the process of experiencing abundance and that pain can be a transformational tool.

I'm here to tell you now that all of the difficulties you experience are transformational tools. Challenges are not "something that just happens," and irritations are not random. They are all purposeful, as each disruption is meant to be your alarm clock, an opportunity for you to remember who you truly are, each a doorway back to Oneness. Difficulties and pain can be utilized as a reminder of the choice that you have to reactivate the frequency of love provided to you when you entered your body at birth.

But pain, for most humans, is not a device for increased consciousness. It has become a landing pad, not an alert system. It has become the end point, and the opportunity to use each difficulty as a transformational tool has been all but lost.

For so many beings and most likely for you, pain is in itself a destination. It's a part of your life that you accept as "just what is." Never questioned, it is something to avoid, to bury, to buy, sex, drink, eat, or drug your way through or out of.

You would likely never think of chaos as helpful or as a tool that could take you to greater awareness, to deeper consciousness, to continual peace, and to the experience of love and connection with each and every being you encounter. But that is exactly its purpose in your life.

In this book I'll be sharing with you profound truths that will challenge your beliefs, rock your foundation, and possibly leave you a bit uncomfortable.

Now, get ready for the most important truth shift of all:

Chaos is here to remind you of who you truly are. You *are love*, higher consciousness, in a physical body. Low frequency events exist in order to provide you a doorway to your highest knowing, enabling you to choose to respond to all of your life from that sacred spot of love.

As you continue to read these chapters, you will discover—and experience for yourself—that you are high-frequency energy that is placed inside of a physical body, and you have a choice every moment of your day to activate your higher consciousness as your response to any difficulty you experience, or not. Please read that again—and again if you need to let its power sink in.

When you choose to respond to low-vibrational experiences from Oneness you completely transmute the frequency of what has arrived in your life. You literally change dark to light, and you begin the journey of reclaiming your gift of peace, neutrality, and abundance.

Imagine what it will be like when you know how to use all of the irritations, difficulties, and challenges that appear in your life as opportunities to respond from love and as tools to build your muscle of tolerance and understanding.

Visualize how meaningful your world will be if what now appears as conflict is truly a moment to create more connection. Think about how peaceful your life will be when you choose to utilize difficulty rather than avoid it.

The teachings in this book will open you to the awareness of the truth of who you are—a high-frequency energy in a dense physical body—and will explain the purpose of pain in your life. The powerful processes I share can be used by you to reaccess, reactivate, and realign your daily life with your higher consciousness, the Oneness, your highest wisdom.

As you are able to utilize the many moments of difficulty that you will experience daily in the physical world as transformational tools, they will remind you to become an expression of your highest frequency once again, and you will indeed begin to create an extraordinary life. This is my promise to you!

Who Are You?

You are not the single "I" that you refer to as yourself.

You are a Lifestream, a multidimensional being filled with *frequencies* that can be simply defined as both high (Oneness, higher consciousness, wisdom, love) and low (fear, judgment, anger, jealousy, lack) energies working within a dense, solid form: your physical body.

If you have any doubt that frequencies are present in your body, remember the medical testing of EEGs and EKGs, tests that measure the frequency of your brain and the frequency of your heart.

In addition, if you are in a hospital at the end of your physical life, you will be attached to a monitor that measures the frequencies of energy in your body and in your brain. When no energy is present, the monitor will record a flat line, and you will be declared deceased. Your body will remain, but your frequency will have moved out.

Frequencies are indeed alive and well inside of you now, and while medical science has acknowledged their presence, most likely you have yet to understand and utilize these powerful aspects of your being as your core directional compass. Yet they are now working moment to moment directing your life, and not always in ways that serve you.

This book empowers you to change the way you now respond in your life and provides you practices that will enable you to choose a high-vibrational response to any event that might occur. Thus you will be creating an exceptional life.

In addition to your frequencies and your physical body, you were gifted a splendid tool called a brain, a highly complex physical organ that oversees your bodily functions and creates, organizes, and structures your frequencies into thoughts and emotional charges that are sent to and through your physical body.

With total respect for the magnificence of this wondrous partner, your life is not (as science and some New Age thinking would have you believe) the total product of your brain. You are more than your brain—so much more!

You are not your thoughts; you are more than that. Your true self is your higher consciousness (Oneness), which to date science has yet to fully explain. But Oneness has been experienced and spoken of since before the beginning of time.

Your brain did not create the Oneness, your higher frequency of consciousness. Oneness is a separate field; it is the energy of love that came into you with your first breath as your brain was activated.

Science has said that the brain does not create anew; rather it recognizes that which already exists. What always exists within you constantly are your energy fields, your high frequency of consciousness, and the low frequency of your egoic mind, which is experienced as pain, lack, judgment, doubt, and worry.

The energy of love and the energy of fear cannot exist at the same time. Just as you cannot be hot and cold concurrently, you cannot hold the energy of love while you experience fear.

As you hold *any* frequency, your brain structures thoughts and emotions around whichever energy field is currently activated.

It is not accurate to say you are your thoughts. It is more accurate to say you are your frequencies. For the frequencies you hold are what your brain creates your emotions and thoughts around.

It is for this reason that *your frequencies—not your thoughts or emotions—should be your guidance system*.

Having the ability to be aware of which frequency you are holding—and shifting your frequencies when they do not serve you—is what is needed in order to respond to difficulty from higher frequencies.

It is not change your thinking, change your life. It is indeed *change your frequency, change your life*, for your thoughts and emotions are a result of the frequency you are holding at any given moment.

The main reason why you have difficulty when trying to change your life habits is because you have been taught to work on the wrong end of the equation. You most likely have been guided to focus your attention on the *result*, not on the *cause*. You are told to try to stop thinking in a certain way or advised to lose emotional patterns that don't serve you.

But thoughts and emotions, as I've pointed out, are the result of the brain structuring around a present energy field. They are not the *cause*. Your energy field is what needs to be shifted, as that's what fuels your brain.

If you are unaware (and most people are) that it's the frequency you hold that needs to change, you will continue to focus your attention on the incorrect part of the equation, and the changes you seek won't occur. But when you start to work with your frequencies and learn how to shift into high-vibrational modes when low frequencies are present, changes occur almost magically—extraordinary changes.

In your earliest days, as you walked in the physical world while your body and brain were developing, so too did your *personality* and *history* mature. Your low and high frequencies were activated and accessed over and over as your responses to life situations.

Frustration as an infant was most likely your first experience with pain. Crying was an announcement that was generated from hunger, from being alone, or from simple discomfort. It was your way of communicating that something was wrong.

Your patterns of response to your life circumstances began at an early age as your humanity began to be influenced by the energy that was present in your physical surroundings. Your family of origin, the beings who took care of you, were your earliest touchstone. Depending on your life circumstances, you may have been exposed to loving kindness or introduced to much pain as your life continued. While a life surrounded by warmth and appreciation and a journey nurtured throughout is indeed most pleasant and what most beings would wish for, it is not the experience many have, and it is not a prerequisite for having an extraordinary life.

Many spiritual students who have found their way to me have had extremely difficult lives, and some became seekers at an early age. They developed a body of knowledge through the readings and workshops they focused their efforts on, but until they took on the work of using the difficulties that appeared in their daily life as their transformational tools, they were still stuck deep inside of each piece of pain they experienced.

How your life manifested in the physical world from the time you were an infant is different from every single being that has been birthed upon our planet. All beings have their own paths, and your life represents no one else's. Your physical body and life patterns are unique, yet you share one quality with everyone else. You contain the identical frequency of Oneness, and you have the same opportunity to experience peace and happiness in an extraordinary life, as do all human beings. These states will indeed be yours to experience as you learn how to respond to the irritations and difficulties that you now experience from one of the many physical manifestations of love.

As a child and as an adult, when you went through any form of loss or fear and you responded in kind, you were choosing to say no to your divinity; you were repeatedly deciding to not access the gift of love that you were seeded with.

Over time, responding to chaos, pain, and loss automatically with more of the same became your habit. You forgot that you had a choice of responses; you did not remember that your highest wisdom was meant to be your GPS system. As you continued to respond from a low frequency, the Oneness got buried in the trunk of your being and your life now reflects this void of remembrance.

If you're like many, the Oneness within you may now only be experienced through occasional, magical moments that you call synchronicity or through prayer and meditation.

When life is easy you feel it's because of "good luck" or karma. When times are tough you may blame others or your own poor thinking. When your health suffers you focus on the illness, believing that putting your attention on the illness itself will heal you. When you lose your job, your home, or a beloved, and you are at loss as to what *to do*, you seek help from teachers and healers, as you do not know how to help yourself.

Whether your life is momentarily disrupted or a present difficulty is a lifelong pattern, it is not surprising that, to you, an easy, peaceful life is something that feels completely out of reach.

Prayer and meditation are helpful tools and healers, and teachers can be beneficial support team members, yet your greatest ally is the Oneness within you; your high frequency is the key to living an extraordinary life. Right now it is lying dormant within you waiting to be reactivated!

The concepts I have put forth here are easy to discuss but may seem difficult for you to implement—unless you have the tools and guidance that I am going to share with you. As a spiritual teacher I've discovered consistent blocks that keep people from leading an extraordinary life, and I've developed key powerful spiritual practices that will move you through each impediment.

As you read on, I will guide you to discover where you are blocked, and then give you tools to open to the Oneness that is your natural gift.

An Extraordinary Life Redefined

When I ask my students what it would look like to live an extraordinary life, they tell me: finding the right romantic relationship, having an overflowing bank account, working in a job that has great meaning, or the return of excellent health.

And when I dig deeper and ask them: Why is a healthy life important? What would a new romantic relationship bring? How would you benefit from a meaningful career? The answer is always the same: "I'd be happy. I'd stop worrying. I'd be at peace."

When I then inquire, *Can you be happy and have peace without your situations changing?* they look at me with a puzzled response and usually become quiet. When I share that long-term peace, happiness, and abundance do not come only from a shift in their external circumstances but can indeed be acquired though altering the frequency of their responses in the small—as well as in the large—moments of their life, most are in disbelief.

I then explain how consciously choosing kindness, compassion, and grace as your reply to daily frustrations and to life's difficulties is what truly enables you to experience peace. While most people agree that walking through life with a positive attitude is helpful, what they miss is how important their moment-to-moment responses to chaos actually are.

Think about the seemingly never-ending frustrations in your life. Is it the scooped subway seat when you are bone tired, or the never-ending traffic jams and the negative vibes you feel on the highways on your way to work? Or maybe it's the person in the "8 Items or Less" line at the grocery store with the overflowing shopping cart when you are running late. Perhaps you are tired of always struggling to pay your bills, and/or going home to a partner who never seems to talk to you anymore. Then there is our world of divisive politics, tremendous poverty, hatred, and injustice, which seem to be endless.

Pick any piece of chaos. It does not matter which you choose; none of them truly represent your short- or long-term peace, for your peace truly lies in the frequency of your response to each one of these difficult situations.

You can't fix the traffic, your partner, the subway seat scooper, or the fast middle finger in the left-hand lane. You can, however, view and use each and every one of these situations as a transformational tool as you learn to choose a response that leaves you at peace and doesn't fuel the situation with even more low frequency.

While you will be learning a bit later in this book how to release frustration in the moment, I'd like to show you, now, how easily you can release low-frequency vibrations from an ordinary or even difficult day.

Nighttime Review

I'm sharing with you an action to take that will help you review your day and give you the opportunity to get into the habit of neutralizing any low frequency that you've created due to your actions, words, or emotions that truly don't serve you or others. It is extremely helpful, as it neutralizes any vibration that you created that you might have missed throughout the day.

ACTION
—✦—
Evening Scan

+ Prepare for bed, and as you're lying down and relaxing, begin to review your day. Start with the morning and allow each experience to pop up. Go through the day trusting that whatever experience is supposed to appear will do so.
+ As you view each situation, note where you were in alignment with your highest frequency and where you were not. Just notice, not allowing yourself to be in judgment of others or yourself or energetically charged in any way by what you see.
+ Remain completely neutral during this review. When you feel this part of the practice is complete, ask the Universe

to neutralize and then release any low frequency that you created due to your thoughts, actions, or words that did not serve.

+ When that piece is complete, begin to visualize the moments of your day that brought you delight. Was it the door that was held for you? The conversation with a favorite neighbor? Or perhaps it was the sunset you witnessed that took your breath away? Whatever your small or large joys were, see each one and feel them again, completely. Then bless yourself and bless the day.

+ Finally, become present to your state. Are you feeling more relaxed? More at ease? Most people report that their anxiety releases and their frustration slips away. This occurs as you have actively chosen to shift frequencies and have brought in the energy of peace.

While your idea on what an extraordinary life looks like might be different from your neighbors', your friends', or your family of origin's, what is shared universally in our culture is the false concept that peace and calm are something outside of you—something that will happen once certain aspects in your life change, or you reach a new level in your spiritual studies.

So many beings seek endlessly to change their circumstances in the quest for happiness, all the time missing the knowledge that peace and joy can be experienced regardless of their external world. If you practiced the Evening Scan, you have already experienced this truth.

The key to your new life lies with the frequency you are holding in each and every moment.

I may already be challenging your view of why your life is or has been filled with pain and not abundance—and now I'm about to redefine what an extraordinary life is.

An extraordinary life is not a destination to reach or a state to achieve. It's an active practice where your daily life is experienced from a consistent state of consciousness and choice. It's a place where you decide to be grateful for what is instead of focusing your attention on what is not. It's you holding neutrality when calm seems a world away. It's you having a sense of peace, of calm, of being filled to the brim regardless of your current state of affairs.

An extraordinary life means you are aware of your present state (frequency) and choose your responses to outside circumstances and events from your highest knowing. For every time you bring in kindness, compassion, and understanding and direct it toward yourself and others, you experience grace.

Your new life doesn't have to be stress free; in fact stressful moments may occur as reminders to bring in more gratitude and equanimity.

This definition of an extraordinary life may not be what you think you have been seeking, and it's most likely not what you currently hold to be true, which is why we're redefining it now.

When we begin, most of my students are functioning from the old paradigm where a great life is represented in their physical world as a plethora of money, as ongoing, excellent health, as professional success, or as the perfect relationship.

You, too, may have automatically accepted this definition. If so, you have been misguided, and your suffering comes from thinking that your peace, happiness, and joy are only possible if these external goals are met.

It's important to share with you that I appreciate that food, shelter, relationships, purposeful employment, and excellent health are certainly valuable aspects of your physical life. Your desire to experience your world in comfort is not at issue. But what does true comfort look like, and how is it achieved?

Take a moment and reflect. Have you known or heard of people who had a great deal of money yet had sad and lonely lives? Were there times in your life where you were in a job that you loved, but you still didn't experience peace? Have you always been happy in a romantic relationship?

There are many wealthy people, or those in great relationships and in optimal health, who still do not experience the peace and equanimity they thought those external qualities of life would bring to them.

While peace, happiness, and joy are states that represent abundance, they don't automatically appear when a bank account is full or health returns, and your new life is not dependent on them being present. External results do not always signify a life led by conscious choice.

Over time, bringing in the energies of kindness, wisdom, and understanding will transform each moment of difficulty. As you transform each instant of pain into love, you energetically in that moment become that frequency.

Eventually your world will reflect in physical form the many choices you made to transform difficulty into grace, and your life will become an expression of peace and neutrality and happiness.

Chaos may never disappear in our world, but by being grounded in high-frequency responses, you'll begin to see your small daily choices begin to shift. You'll experience less drama, you'll choose to let negative people go, and you'll learn to use every bit of difficulty that appears as an opportunity to invoke gratitude. These are actions that will bring you a sense of daily peace.

In this new state of equanimity, you'll begin to sense divinity every-where. You'll experience wonder in your daily life, moment to moment, as you move through your day. *This is an indication that you are liv-ing in a high-frequency state, which creates and attracts to you the very circumstances that you define now as your wishes and your most cherished desires.*

I want to take a moment and check in with you, as the material I'm sharing is deep and profound and requires a great deal of own-ership and responsibility. It is also a jolt to your egoic mind (low-frequency energy field), which until now has most likely totally been running your life.

Absorbing the concepts I'm presenting to you can be challenging. Or the truths I'm sharing may leave you totally excited.

So how are you experiencing the material? As you read the words do you find yourself feeling as if you are with an old friend? Are you sensing a knowing that is deep inside of you, that is waking up and eager to know more?

Or are you uncomfortable, perhaps watching yourself saying, "Baloney. Pain is pain. I can't control my emotions and thoughts. And how does this pay my mortgage and my bills?"

Just take a moment and notice how you are feeling. Then, regardless of what you observed, please keep reading! You've been directed to this book and your continued efforts are the beginning of your actual transformation to peace. Every word you read is energetically reseeding you toward profound change.

My Journey to Living an Extraordinary Life

Before I explain the "how to" of living your extraordinary life, I'd like to briefly share my story. As I write these words, I am about to experience my sixty-fifth birthday, and for the last twenty-five years I have been actively living 24/7 the truths and practices that I'll be sharing with you. While the application of this work started in my daily life when I was in my forties, I was sixteen when Oneness was first introduced to me.

Like many others, I was raised in a family of good people who eventually went through a difficult time that they never seemed to come out of.

As a child I knew that my parents loved me and they worked hard, but I never felt that I belonged to them. My mother seemed to have a tight connection with my sister, and my father with my brother, and I was alone, convinced that I landed in this family by mistake. So much so that at the age of seven, I was continually caught rummaging through my mother and father's drawers looking for my adoption papers!

I was an exceptionally positive and generous child. I frequently gave my possessions to my friends and naturally forgave them when they were unkind to me. My mother, whom I adored, called me a "doormat" when she heard my continual stories of giving my friends my toys and other belongings.

I'm sure she meant well, but I was devastated and felt torn between my natural way of wanting to be generous and seeking my mother's approval. This is my earliest memory of consciously sensing the push and pull of my high- and low-energy systems. Eventually I made choices that represented me leaving behind my generous nature and conforming to the practice of allowing my ego to lead the way, embracing the low vibration of fear that my mother and many others around me modeled and lived within.

As a child I was also incredibly intuitive and empathic. Have you ever been so deeply moved by the pain of others to a point where you could barely hold the suffering you felt them experiencing? That was me.

I remember watching the Muscular Dystrophy Telethon, a televised annual charity event where children who suffered from the illness told their stories and viewers were asked to donate whatever they could. I was old enough to dial a phone but not old enough to understand the implications of that call. All I wanted to do was to be of help. So while crying from the pain of watching the children, I called up and said that I'd send in a five-thousand-dollar donation. When my sister overheard what I had done, she ran to my mother, and my panicked mom called back to let them know that a child had placed that donation and it would not be forthcoming.

By the time I was fourteen my family was a train wreck. My parents had divorced, my dad had moved far away, my fifteen-year-old sister was pregnant, and my mom was rarely home. She worked, went back to grad school, and became extremely involved in the civil rights movement, busy petitioning our local school board on behalf of the NAACP to integrate my high school. This was the beginning of integration, and my mother was a visible presence in our extremely racist community. What she did was brave and noble, but all I knew was that I missed her terribly. I was tired of being beaten up on the way home from school, targeted by bullies in the neighborhood, while within the walls of my home, all eyes were on my sister. Once again I felt alone and for the first time quite unsafe.

Lonely, scared, and broken, I found a lifeline as spiritual teachings were introduced to me by a new group of friends. I devoured the work of Madame Helena Blavatsky and the books of Aleister Crowley. I poured over the *Egyptian Book of the Dead* and began to study tarot and I Ching. Most of the time I didn't understand anything I was reading, but there was a knowing inside of me that the new path I was on was my saving grace.

A year or so later, through a series of divinely given events, I met my first teacher. I was sixteen, and she was a much older woman, a true being of light and a devotee of Master Maitreya, the world teacher of Oneness. She introduced me to the concept of Oneness—of cooperation, not competition. She shared Kabbalistic truths and gave me my name, one that I didn't take fully until many years later: Selina Maitreya. *Selina* means daughter of the moon and mistress of the stars. Completely taken by the romance of the name Selina, I was excited that my new name would indicate my new path. It would be decades and many transformations later until I took the name of Master Maitreya.

The teachings that were shared with me rang true to my core, and I was hungry for more, yet at this point my physical life was still in shambles. I was a totally unformed and fairly dishonest person who was searching desperately to find the kindness, honesty, and joy that I knew was buried deeply within me. Underneath the many experiences of pain, rejection, and loss that I had felt continuously in my childhood was a being of light waiting to emerge. I was confused and extremely lonely, but I was also on a path of discovery.

For the first time in my life the pain I had experienced through my family history and the torment I felt all around because of my empathy were not the only frequencies in my life. As I voraciously read spiritual material I began to consciously experience and note the wonder that began to appear in my world. I was a long way from living my values, but this entrée was a huge awakening.

Fast forward to my early thirties: I was establishing my career as the first marketing consultant to commercial photographers in the United States when I met my husband. I quickly became a wife, mother, published author, successful consultant, and world lecturer. I was hugely busy, and I put my active studies of spirituality on a shelf.

After all, my external life was fabulous and extraordinary in its own way, and I was happier than I had ever been in my life. Why did I need to keep doing the work I had started when I was a miserable teenager?

Seven years later I discovered my mistake. I was unhappy in my marriage, and I once again felt desperate and alone. I had the family I had always wanted, a wonderful house and home, the career that many would kill for, yet I was vacant inside. As my marriage failed, I entered therapy for twelve years, and during that time I was introduced in a most magical way to my current spiritual teacher, Rev. Janice Hope Gorman.

One day, early in our work together, Hope mentioned Maitreya and the teachings of Oneness that had been my lifeline when I was sixteen years old. I cannot begin to tell you how awed I was that once again, in a time of desperation, Spirit reached out to me through the teachings of Oneness.

Twenty-seven years later I was once again working with the same truths, but this time I wasn't just *reading* about how to be a spiritual person; with Hope's guidance I was actively transforming the expressions of fear in my life into the frequencies of kindness, compassion, and understanding. I was *living* the principles of Oneness.

I was using my daily life, watching my behavior, monitoring my frequencies, and shifting into higher vibrational responses when I felt fear of any kind.

And fear was ever present as I moved through a painful divorce, took on the majority of financial responsibility for my two boys, and worked twelve-hour days as a mom, consultant, author, and lecturer for the next fifteen years.

And Oneness was always my guide.

I used all of the tools that I'll be sharing with you, and they are truly the reason that I was (and still am) able to feel blessed every day, even though I was often bone tired, financially challenged, and alone. But loneliness was never my experience because I truly felt the presence of grace and was continually steeped in gratitude as I had learned to *become* the frequencies of compassion and understanding.

These states did not magically appear; they were indeed a result of my continually using the many difficulties I faced daily as reminders to respond from love. I have had numerous opportunities to practice all of what I am sharing with you.

Every time I chose to actively remember who I was and made the decision to reactivate the Oneness inside of my being, I began to experience happiness and true peace, regardless of what chaos landed in my life.

Now I continually choose a response of kindness, patience, understanding, and tolerance when I feel judged, disregarded, or ignored. I choose gratitude when I feel I'm in lack, and I choose grace when I forget who I truly am and am unkind to others.

I opt to use all daily irritations and difficulties as they appear as opportunities to respond from my highest knowing.

It is my consistent practice of not responding to chaos with more of the same, but rather using it as a transformational tool, that has created a truly extraordinary life.

As I write these words, I'm totally excited for you, as I know that your life will be completely transformed as you put into practice the information I share with you.

In the next chapters you will learn how to align your new beliefs and your actions. I will share with you blind spots my students often experience, and I will provide you with transformational goals and actions that will empower you to use all difficulties you encounter as a transformational tool. From this moment on, each and every irritation you experience, every perceived slight, hurt, and inconvenience, is now yours to use to build a life of equanimity and peace, an extraordinary life that will indeed be represented by you manifesting the wishes and desires you have long held.

Now, it is your turn. Read on and begin to create your extraordinary life.

2

Shift the Paradigm

Transformational Goal: *Discover Where You Are Now*

A s I begin to guide you through the amazing shift to living an extraordinary life for yourself, of responding to all events from your intuitive body and your higher wisdom rather than from your egoic mind (and its history of pain) or a low-frequency emotional state, you must dig a bit deeper and take an inventory of your current Lifestream. We start with the practice of awareness, where you notice your state instead of being inside of it without any observation at all.

Developing Awareness

While there are many frequencies within you, two main energy fields are the source of your experience every moment of your day. They are the low-level egoic field, experienced in the physical world as fear, which shows up as resistance, lack, intolerance, anger, jealousy, procrastination, and judgmental thoughts; or the high frequency of love that manifests as an extraordinary life filled with kindness, compassion, understanding, wisdom, tolerance, patience, gratitude, grace, and peace.

Having an awareness as to which "body" or energy field, and what specific manifestations of that field, you currently and repeatedly access will change your life as you begin to notice and identify your states as they come into form.

This knowledge is pivotal as it begins to create a level of recognition within you that you are indeed a multidimensional being. Ultimately you will be able to experience the different energy fields you occupy at any given moment as separate entities rather than seeing yourself as a singular "I," which is most likely your experience right now!

Being able to identify which energy frequency is currently active will also be extremely helpful information to return to when I teach you how to recognize and experience any current state while inside the moment of an experience, which is a pivotal key to you being able to transform any type of fear into love.

ACTION

◆

Initial Inventory

As you take this assessment, please do so with kindness, and as best you can please leave your judgment (a low-frequency energy in itself) behind. Should you notice that you are feeling angry or disappointed as you answer the questions below, use this moment as your first opportunity to transform your low frequency into higher realms by breathing out the low vibration and taking in another breath into grace.

As you answer the four sets of questions below, specific to each of your four bodies—emotional, intellectual, egoic, and intuitive—think about events in the last few weeks.

1. How often have you been responding from your emotional energy field?
   - Is anger a common response when you do not feel appreciated or loved?

- Are you jealous of others, wondering why your life's dreams are still not yet fulfilled?
- Do you experience anxiety, or are you concerned about money or your health?
- Have you noticed that you have a short fuse and are reactive when others are unkind to you?

2. Now, review how often you have been responding from your intellectual energy field.
   - Do you have a really active brain that never seems to slow down?
   - Is multitasking your way of life?
   - Do you thrive on writing lists and accomplishing every item?
   - Are meditation and sleep almost impossible because your brain is always busy?
   - Do you love to organize and structure your day, your work, and your life, and do you always want others in your world to be more organized?
   - Do you feel that every occurrence needs to be logically explained?

3. Now take a look at how often you have been responding from your egoic body.
   - Do you find yourself a harsh judge of others and of yourself?
   - Do you have the need to make yourself right and others wrong?
   - After an emotional charge, do you find yourself creating stories after each perceived slight and insult?
   - Do you sit inside the stories, repeating them over and over to yourself and to anyone who will listen?
   - Do you find yourself being competitive, often comparing yourself to your friends and family and strangers you don't know?

4. Finally, review your intuitive body. How often have you been responding from your intuitive energy field?
   - Do you experience a sense of Oneness with all beings?

- Are you able to experience hurt, pain, and grief and respond with patience, kindness, and understanding?
- Have you chosen to surround yourself with people who move through the world with positivity and grace, choosing to leave drama behind?
- Is your life filled with deep purpose and meaningful connections?
- Are you able to manifest your wishes and desires?
- Do you feel abundant regardless of your circumstances?

This initial inventory is vitally important, and these questions will give you greater insight into which energy fields you currently inhabit most frequently. It will serve you well to take a moment to explore how all of your responses in the last few weeks have created your current state.

As you are energy in form, all of your energy fields—from the emotional to the intellectual to the egoic mind and through to the intuitive—are valuable and useful. However, historically your emotional body and egoic mind most likely have been totally running the show. What did you discover? Be gentle with yourself, as you may never have been introduced or encouraged to activate your intuitive body, and your life may now be a representation of the lack of divinity and Oneness that you are hungry for. The good news is that you have been drawn to the teachings in this book, and clearly you are ready to make the shift!

How It All Began

As I shared in chapter 1, when you entered your physical body upon birth, you were Source energy incarnated into physicality. The Oneness, your intuitive body (the physical manifestation of Source energy), was alive and well, and in addition to your caregivers' love, it was your greatest comfort and your identity.

Why do babies receive so much attention? Why are most people so instinctively drawn to them? It's because all they are is the frequency of love in a warm, tiny body. What you sense in the presence of each newborn is the essence of the Divine.

While you may not have a conscious awareness that this is the reason for the attraction, you are in that moment being energetically reminded of the core of Oneness that you hold buried deep within your own Lifestream.

When you were newly born and you began to develop within the physical world, as your brain was activated and your emotional system engaged, you immediately began to respond to life from the emotional and intellectual bodies within your multidimensional being, and they then were sourced with high frequency.

That's all you knew; that is all you were.

As you grew into your body and your brain developed, you began to have exchanges with the people in your life. Your genetic makeup and family of origin in this incarnation contributed to the experiences you had.

When you experienced love and pain, your emotional body responded to all you were going through. Your thoughts were generated by your emotional responses, and your feelings then generated new thoughts. All of the thoughts and emotions created were physical expressions of the frequencies you were experiencing.

But as you didn't know about your frequencies, your identification was solely with your emotions and thoughts, all described by you as "me" or "I," a one-dimensional being referenced as "self." The loss of your intuitive body was underway.

Your true self is a higher frequency, one that is called love, and it actuates in physical form as your intuitive body. Every expression of kindness, compassion, or understanding that you receive or share activates this field.

Conversely, every painful experience and each act that is not loving builds the low frequency of fear (egoic mind) and generates a new pattern of response that repositions your intuitive body further from your reach.

Over the years, as your Lifestream grew due to social conditioning, your original frequency of love began to be replaced with more experiences of fear and any lack that you encountered. Depending on your circumstances, your shift from being energetically fueled by your highest frequency of love to being guided by fear happened at a very early age.

As you continued your journey, your capacity to "think" was hugely valued by all around you. When you were young and your parents and teachers were pleased with your choices, you were praised for "thinking well." When they were not happy with your behavior, you were asked, "Whatever were you thinking?"

The emphasis on your thinking ability combined with the ever-increasing experience of fear crowded the field, and your intuitive body of Oneness had little room for existence.

You saw "you" as one singular being, where your intuitive body had no place. While it still existed inside your Lifestream it was accessed less and less until it was forgotten.

While higher energetic fields never leave your Lifestream, in order for them to be actualized *you must choose to access them*. Think of your energetic fields as your muscles. Muscles exist within your body; they never go away. But they do strengthen or atrophy depending on your activities.

As you choose to use your biceps or triceps they grow stronger and become more visible. A day or so after a heavy workout you may notice that your muscles are aching. If you keep exercising they grow stronger and you are able to sustain longer periods of practice. Over time you are in peak shape. But if you rarely engage in physical activity, your muscles are present but you won't see them and they certainly won't be toned. When you go to use them you'll find that you are working very hard to do very little because your muscles have been dormant and can't sustain much activity. In the early days it takes a lot of effort for you to continue to work out because at this stage you don't see progress and all you experience is the pain of sore muscles. Your intuitive body is no different. If you don't access it, it too becomes a hidden part of you waiting to be called to action!

From the time you were an infant you accessed your high-energy field of Oneness and love less and less until it became dormant. Your low frequency, your egoic and intellectual minds, were your GPS, and as you called upon them they grew stronger. As we live in a society that overidentifies with the logical brain, it is no surprise that you are intellectually driven, as well.

Now your egoic body and your intellect are in control, and your higher intuitive body is waiting to be rediscovered and strengthened.

You were conditioned at an early age to believe that you are your thoughts and you are your emotions, end of story. With that truth being all you knew, your emotions (thoughts moving through your body) became your landing pad, the final resting place after emotionally charged events occurred. You sat inside the anger, inside the pain, the disappointment, and the rage. As you sat there deep inside the low frequency of your egoic body, you energetically gave it life and fueled it more and more. And that muscle became stronger.

You were never trained to fully experience low-level energy and then respond to it with actions that represent higher frequency vibrations.

Instead, you were taught to hold tightly to all perceived hurts, insults, and pain or to bury them deeply within. You might even have been taught to respond with more pain, an "eye for an eye." Your thoughts and emotions became all you knew, and battle scars built upon each other, adding to the history and content that the egoic mind rehashed over and over in your Lifestream, directing the next moment in time from a position of past painful events.

All the while your intuitive body, the Oneness in you, where your capacity to create the abundance of an extraordinary life lies, was waiting to be called into action.

You were never told that your emotions are driven by an energy field within your Lifestream. All you knew was what you felt. No one explained that scary or worrisome thoughts were the product of a low frequency that you could change. You simply toughed out the difficult moments, waiting for them to go away.

Never were you informed that low and high energies existed, nor were you taught that you had the power to shift them at any time. But you do!

Often I find that as I begin to work with my students, they can't imagine not being worried, losing their anxiety, or dropping the negative judgment of themselves and of others that has become as automatic as their breath. But soon after they begin to witness their energy fields and start to respond to pain from their higher frequency—the intuitive body—they notice visible changes. They relish in the joy of experiencing the choice they never knew they had, the option to respond to pain from love. They undergo an immediate aha moment as they use that choice to shift their state, not accepting pain as their final destination.

Over time their lives become a full expression of their efforts as they begin to experience peace around people and situations that before represented great difficulty. These are the experiences that I know you, too, will have as you begin to put the practices I'm sharing into place.

The Intuitive Body and Egoic Mind Cannot Exist in the Same Space

Your intuitive body, your higher knowing, was always meant to be your guidance system in your daily life.

Your thoughts and emotions were meant to act as a team, to work in tandem alerting the Lifestream to needed information, in order to provide you with the tools you needed to actualize your higher purpose, responding to all in your life from love.

Your thoughts and emotions were meant to support the intuitive body as it guided you through your life, not the other way around.

Just as you cannot be hot and cold at the same time, the egoic mind cannot exist in the same space as the intuitive body. At some point early in your development your intuitive body became inactive as your egoic mind became ever powerful. Each time you activated the egoic mind, your intuitive body quietly moved from the driver's seat to the passenger seat and then was locked in the trunk of your being, rarely accessed as a response to daily life situations.

At this point, your divinity was no longer your guide, and your egoic mind, fueled by your emotions and thoughts, became your lead, your internal usher. What you thought was what you knew yourself to be. If your emotional state was peaceful it was a good day, but if your thoughts turned to worries and concerns, suddenly your life was nothing more than your troubled mind. This sounds familiar, doesn't it?

Your momentary state was how you viewed the world and was controlled and directed by your past thoughts and emotions. You felt your life was also controlled by the actions of others and the external chaos that revolved around you—and this became what you reacted to. As others around you followed the same path, you believed that this was how life was supposed to be.

Over time, your Lifestream, your thinking brain, your egoic mind, and your emotional body all blended seamlessly into the one that you continued to call "I." Your intuitive body had no place in this paradigm. It was completely left behind, and it is still in the trunk of your being, deeply buried until you choose to bring it out.

During the course of your lifetime you have developed patterns for coping that rely on the thinking brain and on your emotions. Your response to everything you experience is generated and filtered through one of these two bodies. Your Source energy, your intuitive body, that which sustained you in your earliest days, is not being utilized as it was meant to be: your moment-to-moment automatic system for response. You no longer access your true self, the intuitive body, on a regular basis.

You may have moments when your intuitive body is activated. Perhaps you were thinking of another person and they contacted you. Or you have a memory of something that you feel has happened before, but it's not quite clear and then that experience shows up in your life. You call these moments synchronicity, not understanding that you are being offered a tiny glimpse into the world of wonder that is waiting to awaken within you and create your extraordinary life one choice at a time.

Even if you have been studying spiritual material or meditating and praying for some time, and you have the knowledge that your intuitive body exists, it most likely is still not your go-to frequency, and your life represents this unfortunate truth.

I'd like to share a story that happened to me many years ago. This story represents how easy it is to lose your center—even when you are well along a spiritual path—if your intuitive body is not yet your daily guidance system.

As a mother of two small boys and the owner of a business that I loved, I led an extremely full life and was always busy. At the point of this story, I had been a spiritual student for twenty years, and I knew that I had yet to fully integrate all of what I had learned into my life.

My daily practice of meditation was one of the few points of access where I was able to connect with my higher self completely. Oh, how I valued that marvelous gift!

One day, while at home with my two young boys, I was stressed and desperately needed to meditate. I asked my sons to do some quiet tasks or activities, as I was going to meditate in a room that was on the other side of the door to their playroom. They quickly agreed, and I was grateful for their cooperation. I shut the door and began to go into stillness—and then I heard loud noises, lots of laughter, and the sound of small bodies being thrown onto the door.

I pulled myself from the depths back into reality, leaned out the door, and gently reminded my boys that I was trying to meditate.

Once again, they guaranteed me that they understood and would do something less disruptive. After shutting the door one more time, I began to relax, to breathe, to go deep, and as soon as I started to calm my body and mind, I once again heard lots of laughter, much shouting, and wrestling taking place.

Without a moment's thought or hesitation, I went from a deep state of peace, leapt out of my chair, threw open the door, and proceeded to scream at the top of my voice at my two little boys. Instantly, my emotional body had taken over, and whatever peace and calm I had experienced was gone in a flash!

My boys were extremely shocked and horribly scared, wondering where their mother had gone and who was this imposter in her place? I wondered the very same thing.

At that point of my life, my higher knowing was not grounded in my physicality, and I was unable to retain a calm state the second time the boys interrupted my meditation. As we can't retain high frequency at the same time we experience low frequency, the low energy had more presence and I ended up screaming.

My story is your story, too, as your emotional body and egoic mind continue to be your past and current history, ready to be activated in a millisecond of perceived pain. They are now your main response mechanisms that you automatically employ when you feel discomfort of any kind.

To reiterate: as high and low frequency cannot be present at the same time, when you impulsively react from your historical, emotional state fueled by your egoic mind, there is no room for your intuitive body to be present, and so there is little chance for peace.

Creating Space between Event and Response

If you recognized a variation of yourself in my story, then right now for you there is only event and reaction.

What you must learn—and what reading and working with the practices in this book will help you to achieve—is your first step in creating an extraordinary life: *You must create a space in between your experience and your response; in that space lies your ability to choose to respond to any life circumstance from one of the many physical manifestations of love.*

Please read that sentence over and over, as it is a key piece of your new knowledge. When you learn to create space between an event and your response, you are able to choose the frequency you wish to respond from rather than responding unconsciously from the same (low) frequency of the energy presented to you. This is when you can begin to access your highest frequency and have the gift of experiencing the freedom of conscious choice!

When you are able to choose patience, kindness, gratitude, compassion, understanding, tolerance, and wisdom as your reaction, even when in the midst of a highly charged moment, then you are creating peace and developing—and living—an extraordinary life!

Life Experiences That Keep You from Accessing Your Intuitive Body

Being able to stay in a state of loving response and/or being emotionally neutral is key to experiencing peace. Peace is an expression of your activated higher frequencies and is in itself a physical expression of abundance.

And you, dear reader: where and when do you lose your center? Does your world shift quickly as your emotional states change? Is there, for you, a sense of self beyond your thoughts and emotions, or are you just a bundle of feelings and reactions? Are there people with whom you are in daily contact that you feel emotionally charged by: a parent, child, sibling, coworker, or a neighbor to whom you find it hard to have a neutral or loving response?

Take a moment and become aware of who these beings are. You might find yourself saying: My mother drives me crazy. My neighbor is so inconsiderate. My partner doesn't appreciate me. My children are so thoughtless.

The words you use—*thoughtless, inconsiderate, crazy*—represent the judgments that you hold, and they are your keys to discovering the relationships that you can choose to work with as you accept responsibility for your current emotional and egoic responses.

The second, vitally important step for you to take after creating a space between your experience and your response is: ***Accept total responsibility for all of the events and exchanges that come into your life and use your current responses and actions as your transformational tools. No one is doing anything to you. You are being given events and exchanges to work with in order to practice how to have a loving response to all.***

That is one of the true purposes of the disharmony that is currently active in your life. I know this is a profound concept that shakes your world. But accepting this truth and working with it will lead to the peace that you seek. Yes, ***you have been given each experience in order for you to remember to be who you truly are.*** You are love, and your intuitive body is calling to be reinstated as your moment-to-moment response mechanism. Each time you use the practices I will be sharing with you to transform your low-frequency energy into love, you will be accessing your intuitive body and it will grow stronger, just like your muscles.

When you respond to any sort of difficulty from a manifestation of love, you are accessing the Oneness within you that is waiting to be reactivated!

Consistent Physical World Triggers

In addition to specific relationships in life, there may be certain situations that keep you from accessing your intuitive body and lead to you losing your center. Consider the questions below and begin to identify any specific patterns or life situations that you consistently react to with more chaos.

- Do you feel stressed when you are in a rush to get somewhere and others are moving slowly? Do you have less patience for others and yourself when you are tired or hungry?

- Perhaps you lose your center and snap when waiting endlessly for your call to be connected to a service provider, or you are trying to straighten out a mistake that has been made and the person you are speaking with just isn't hearing your request?
- Is it stressful for you to sit down and attempt to pay your bills, especially as it seems as if there is never enough money to go around?
- Is someone at work always leaving a mess behind and you are tired of cleaning up after them?
- Do you have health issues that you need to address and the health system seems to be working against you?
- Are you experiencing constant pain or physical ailments?
- Perhaps your perfect partner still has not arrived, and you find yourself tired of having to be patient?

I know that the difficulties you experience now may not feel like gifts to you. And be assured I am not glossing over your current situation and asking you to immediately see your world through different eyes. I *am* offering, however, a new proven and realistic way of living your life. And I'm providing you with the steps to take in order to affect the change you long to truly make to become the calm, peace-filled, and grateful being who gets to live an extraordinary life.

Difficulties, stress, and tragedies are a part of life. Should you *not* use them as opportunities to learn how to respond from a higher frequency, all you will be left with is the pain and chaos of each life event. Thus, I encourage you to begin to see all difficulties as spiritual instruments for your increased consciousness on your journey back to Oneness and the extraordinary life you so deserve!

These truths are simple to read, and I trust you are feeling excited as you recognize what has been buried deep inside of you. Please remember that you will need to practice your new way of being, moment to moment, as is true when learning any new skill. So let's get started!

What follows is the first step that will help you to turn any difficulty into peace.

ACTION

———◆———

Observe Your Difficult Daily Events with Neutrality

The purpose of this exercise is to help you to bring your *awareness* to the variety of emotional charges and negative thoughts you currently experience. Awareness is the first step toward using difficulty as a vehicle for your transformation into openness and Oneness. Noting which people and circumstances currently move you off center will help you as we progress.

The tool of observation that you are employing in this simple exercise of taking inventory of where you are is your first opportunity to practice your new way of walking in your world. Start now, and do not hold yourself in harsh judgment as you take the review below. Simply answer the questions with an open heart, staying in a place of *gentle and genuine inquiry*. This is important to note, for as you remain in curiosity while reviewing the questions, you are actively working from your intuitive body (an open state) not from your egoic mind, which is in judgment (a closed state).

1. Who are the people in your life that you feel the most negative emotional charge around?
2. Note a recent time when you felt charged by one of them.
3. In what situations do you find your emotions are on high alert? At work? On the highway home? With neighbors?
4. Note a recent experience with a nonfamily member or friend when you responded from a highly charged, negative emotional state.
5. Are there times that your physical state contributes to your emotional surges? Do hunger, cold, and lack of sleep affect your sense of peace?
6. Do you find yourself blaming others for your current state?
7. Who or what do you misidentify most as "responsible" for your lack of peace?
8. Have you gotten angry, disappointed, or "let down" by others?

9. Note a situation that represents your feeling let down or disrespected by someone.

You needn't answer or work with all nine questions above. Know that the questions you are drawn to now are where you should begin. This work is not a test. These questions and practices are provided at this point to help you to see the relationships and situations that have been given to you, in this journey of yours, to work with as you move forward creating the paradigm shift into living life from your intuitive body.

As you review your responses, note the people in your life who you seem to hold in judgment and who you feel judged by.

List for yourself the states you experience when you are more apt to respond with an emotional response or negative thoughts.

When you have completed the questions regarding others, take some time and notice what actions you have taken in the past that created the urge to harshly judge yourself.

This piece of your work is extremely important, as often my students find it much easier to see where they are in conflict around others, yet rarely notice the many times they harshly judge themselves.

As you answer the questions above from a place of observation rather than from judgment of yourself, you are already beginning the process of aligning your actions with your values of responding to life from love.

This system I am sharing with you of using your judgments to signal an opportunity to go to grace will eventually become second nature. The energetic vibrations created from your newly integrated self will open the doorway to an entirely new series of wondrous events.

This is what I call "neutral observation," and it takes a bit of work. You may see yourself getting agitated as you notice that you are constantly energetically negatively charged when you interact around your neighbor. Perhaps you begin to feel depressed as you remember shouting at your children when you were tired or hungry.

As you begin to see or feel your body react to your behavior, immediately note this, then breathe and remind yourself that you are in the process of creating the shift you need! Then move! Use Steps for Going to Grace below to bring yourself back to neutrality.

ACTION

———◆———

Steps for Going to Grace

✦ Notice the judgmental thought or feeling toward yourself or another you are experiencing.

✦ Take a deep breath, then speak the words: "Cancel that! Cancel that!" Imagine yourself pulling a plug out of the wall, ending the charge.

✦ View yourself surrounded by a great ball of light and say out loud: "I am light, I am love."

✦ Feel these words of grace in your body. Sense your body becoming lighter, and feel in your body the love that you truly are.

✦ Repeat this practice as many times as needed until you begin to feel relaxed and at ease.

This practice could easily be dismissed by your egoic mind as too simple to be effective, but please resist any urge to let your ego convince you of that. This practice is a simple yet extremely powerful tool. Here's how it works:

You *are* energy, so it is critical that you cancel the low energetic vibration created whenever you begin to chastise others or see yourself in a negative light. Saying "Cancel that!" immediately and powerfully ends the low vibration you have created. It's like pulling the cord out of the wall and ending an electric charge, and you will feel it immediately.

When you say "I am light, I am love," you are moving your being from a low frequency to a high frequency. In addition, you are affirming energetically in the physical world in which you live that you are indeed light.

Experiencing the words of grace, "I am light, I am love," in your body is the access point for your energy fields to shift. As you are an energetic generator as well as a transmitter, your words carry powerful vibrations. This simple practice is indeed quite potent as it creates energetic equanimity.

The system I am sharing with you, of using your judgments to signal an opportunity to go to grace, will become second nature. The energetic vibrations created from your newly integrated self will open the doorway to an entirely new series of wondrous events that come from activating the Oneness residing in your Lifestream.

When Do You Currently Access Your Highest Vibration?

I recognize that life does not only contain moments that can be categorized as onerous, difficult, and demanding. You most certainly experience joy, tranquility, and deeply connected moments. As I help you to begin your shift by identifying your states as the multidimensional "you" who walks through the world, it is imperative that you consciously recognize the times when you *do* work from your intuitive body.

Knowing whom you easily give love to, and understanding in which life situations you are able to be patient, kind, and compassionate, provides your first clues as to where and when you now bring in your divine essence of Oneness. Noting the experiences you've already had working from wisdom and grace will give you opportunities to revisit these states more often on a daily basis.

ACTION
———◆———
Take Inventory of You!

As you answer the questions below, please use your power of observation and leave your judgments behind.

1. Who are the people or animals in your life you feel unconditional love for?

2. Who do you feel loves you unconditionally?

3. Was there a recent time when you felt you received unconditional love?

4. In what situations does your Lifestream feel most at ease? At work? Home? With friends? With an animal companion? In nature?

5. Has there been a recent experience with a family member or at work when chaos or drama was happening around you, yet you were able to remain neutral?

6. When do you find yourself more able to be loving to others? When you are: Rested? Warm? Financially sound? Feeling loved and appreciated?

7. Do you find yourself needing others to be kind to you first before you extend yourself to them?

8. Who or what do you credit most for your sense of peace?

9. When are you able to be excited for others? Are you truly happy for them when they share their accomplishments and success?

10. How often do you hear yourself speak well of yourself?

11. Are the people you choose to be with supportive of your efforts and your dreams?

12. What percentage of your life finds you delighted, joyous, serene, content, living in gratitude, and at peace?

This review has given you the opportunity to practice observation without judgment and has provided a window into who you are now. You have already begun the journey into the field of ongoing peace and equanimity as you have reviewed your current states, reviewed relationships that challenge you, and noticed when you easily love and inhabit your intuitive body. Keep your answers handy because you will use them later in the book.

I'd like to share a success story about a student who has been on the path to creating an extraordinary life, the very same one you are on.

LESLIE'S STORY

Moving from Judgment to Unconditional Love

Leslie always experienced a deep, spiritual connection to his higher self from an early age. He naturally engaged in spiritual thinking for years and had worked at a high level of expressing love on a daily basis. Known as an extremely generous man who simply resonated kindness and grace, he still experienced a disconnect between his value of knowing that he was love and his ability to live inside of that truth during challenging moments with his mother.

A devoted son, he had many wonderful years and memories with his loving mother, who had worked very hard to provide a home for him and his brother in a new country after they fled the place where he was born. As he became successful in his career, his mother retained her place as an important part of his world. He appreciated visiting her, sharing her wonderful cooking, and experiencing her joy as she sang and danced around her apartment.

As she grew older, she became afflicted with dementia, and Leslie, ever devoted, put his career on hold to help his mother. As he began to care for her and she fell deeper into the illness, her once carefree, openhearted way of being began to shift, and over time her behavior turned into unfathomably painful experiences, as she was often verbally abusive. She needed continued assurances, and her repeated phone calls to him several times a day often required him to stop whatever he was doing to take a ninety-minute trip to her home in order to calm her down and soothe her worries.

He did this at first quite willingly—and openheartedly—always reminding himself that her behavior was a product of her illness and was not who she was. Over the years watching his finances deplete, his career options dwindle, and his personal life unravel due to her necessary care, and continually being the recipient of her anger, pain, and delusions, he forgot who she was, and he simply shut down to her. He found himself shouting back, being irritated and short-tempered and withholding his love from his mother.

While Leslie's response would seem like a "normal" reaction, it was not in alignment with his natural state of love. ***In addition to the pain from his mother's behavior, what truly affected his core was the pain he was inflicting upon both of them whenever he responded to her from outside of the vibration of love.***

This energetic cycle continued to progress with daily life becoming unbearable. Then one day almost in a flash, Leslie realized that his relationship with his mother was a gift and his biggest opportunity for his own spiritual transformation.

He recognized that he needed to find his path back once again to loving responses, regardless of what her conduct looked like. Below, he talks about the palpable shift in his relationship with his mother once he began to again respond to her from love.

> *Dealing daily with my mother's dementia created a tremendous amount of tension between the two of us. Nothing I did seemed to ameliorate the situation. That is, until I realized that the main reason for the tension between us was because I was not seeing her for who she was beyond her present behavior. I was in distress, missing the mother I knew and used to have, and I was responding to her from that pain.*
>
> *Once I started to see beyond her present form and remembered who she truly was, a loving being I treasured, I was able to shift from reacting with annoyance to interacting with her, as well as myself, with more patience, kindness, and compassion.*
>
> *As I treated her more gently, she became less irritated with me, and I in turn found her less difficult. That simple shift has had, and continues to have, a major impact in our daily interactions.*

Her treatment of him still continued to fluctuate, and while he experienced pain, he knew to use it as an "alarm clock" to remind himself that a loving response was called for. What Leslie accomplished was to offer his mother true acceptance, which many refer to as unconditional love.

Instead of allowing his mother's actions, *the local chaos*, to engage his emotional body and egoic mind and direct his response, he used her behavior to remind himself to choose a loving response, and he would activate his intuitive body and respond to her fear with love.

In the process of finding his way back to loving responses with his mother, Leslie had been reminded that loving care needed to be applied to himself as well. Thus, he was always working from the state of love.

Once Leslie was able to create the shift (from low frequency to high response), opportunities to create space in his life appeared, and he was ready to receive them. He was able to begin to rebuild his career and personal life—steps that were only able to happen after he *cleared the distraction of the chaos* that he and his mother had been inside of for years!

Leslie's story is also a wonderful example of what I speak of when I say that the energy of fear that manifests as anger, unkindness, and intolerance carries a different vibration than the energy of love and that different results occur when you transform fear into love.

This is an ideal time to remind you that the work you do here is not just directed outward from your Lifestream to others, but that you are called to direct the energy of love to your own Lifestream. The energy of Oneness, the high-vibrational essence that lives within you, can only be activated by you, for you, to experience in your physical world. Of course in the Oneness of all that exists, your frequency experienced is on one level, experienced by all. What follows is a gift to give yourself, a reminder of who you truly are, as you take this exceptional journey.

Become the Receiver of Your Grace

You have come here, seeded with free will and the gift of choice. You are given this in order to have the opportunity to activate the Oneness of who you are at any given moment. With this knowledge, give the gift of love to your being every moment of every day!

Remember to grace your Lifestream with kindness, patience, under-standing, and compassion. Become aware of all of the opportunities you have been given and sit with gratitude for all that you are. Take time during your day to physically review the wonderful qualities that exist within you that are both human and Divine.

Take great pleasure in noting your kindness, your generosity of heart, your compassionate nature, your keen thinking abilities, and your miraculous physical body. This may be the most difficult practice for you, for I see that many beings on our planet rarely if ever sit and appre-ciate who they are.

To review: the difficulties you experience in your physical world are given to you as opportunities to activate and share the essence of the Oneness, the essence of love that is within you, with others. As you reactivate your higher frequency and begin to share the energy of love with all, you are continually reseeded with that vibration.

It can be no other way.

When you are not capable of giving love to others, give love to your-self. Forgive yourself for not being able to be of service or of kindness. Do not get trapped in the distraction of guilt. For every situation is an opportunity to turn to love, and if you are not able to be in loving response to another, give yourself that love.

Directing the frequency of love to yourself manifested as patience, compassion, and understanding would seem to be a natural step. Often as I begin to work with my students I see few of them giving themselves grace. Is this your first step?

Have you forgotten that you are at your core nothing more than love? How can you begin to hold love in response to others if you have denied yourself this precious gift for so long?

After reading about your multidimensional qualities and observing where you are now, I trust that you are excited about the next step in turn-ing all chaos that lands in your world into physical manifestations of love!

Having this knowledge of your current state is the first step toward creating an extraordinary life. But knowledge needs to be applied in the physical world in order for it to be transformational. One of my favorite sayings that Spirit delivered to me speaks to this fact: ***Knowledge actualized becomes experience. Experience repeated becomes wisdom.***

Knowing that knowledge needs to be actualized in the physical world in order for it to be realized, I have deliberately created this book filled with actions directly relating to the knowledge shared. Even if you are not seeing any changes now, as you take each action you *are* creating your shift from living in fear to living from love, and you are becoming more energetically and physically abundant! You are now creating your extraordinary life!

There is no greater opportunity to connect knowledge to action than by aligning your spiritual beliefs with your daily actions. The most common block to living a life of deep connection and peace is the lack of consistently living out your truths.

In the next chapter you will be able to see when you are aligned with your spiritual truths . . . and when you are not.

3

Change Your Frequency, Change Your Life!

Transformational Goal: *Realign Your Values and Actions*

Y ou now know that your emotions and thoughts are a product of the frequency you are holding and that you have free will, which enables you to choose to shift your frequency any time you wish.

Sit with that new belief and feel its power!

You can now have freedom from your emotional pain and past history. Current world tragedies and difficult personal events no longer need to hover and cloud your daily life. Assumptions, perceptions, and perceived slights that were your triggers before, sending you into deep spirals of worry, doubt, and regret, no longer need apply. Sitting inside moments you regard as hurtful and painful will be a thing of the past.

You now know that you and you alone are in charge of whether you will live an extraordinary life or not. But having this knowledge does not shift your habitual patterns. You have work ahead of you in order to shift this knowledge into true experience.

A quick review: You have been trained since your birth to respond to life from lack, which manifests as fear, and over time you have adopted the habit of expecting the worst and feeling "lucky" when life went your way. You did not know that the many small moments in your life and your vibrational responses to them created your next moment, leading you to peace or worry.

But now you do.

Everything Is Frequency!

As you are now choosing to shift the paradigm from living in old, low-frequency habits and embracing a new, extraordinary lifestyle, one where you are grounded in your high energy of love, equanimity, and abundance, you will need to learn how, moment by moment, to change your frequency in order to change your life.

I'm excited you are taking this step with me! You've chosen to be on this exciting journey, and I am honored to guide you as you begin to use every difficulty in your life as an opportunity to experience peace.

As you experienced in chapter 2, your first step on this path is to be present to your state and then choose to shift it when it does not serve your higher good. This will require effort and discipline and specific tools. That's why you are here now. You are ready to take on the work of learning how to become aware of which frequency you're in at any moment and then shift it at will.

I am told His Holiness the Dalai Lama is a perfect example of one who has mastered the art of actualizing this truth into his life. Years ago, a friend of mine was the photographer for the Dalai Lama. In order to capture images of him she would position herself in the front row as he gave his teachings. She said that his face was constantly in motion. You could see him consistently shifting his frequencies; his thoughts and emotions were right there on his face as he experienced and released them, making way for the next moment, thought, and reaction.

Clearly, you do not need to become as practiced as the Dalai Lama before you are able to shift your frequencies, but you will need to do some heavy lifting. I encourage you to take on this effort with joy and wonder, for you now know that when you change your frequency you change your life, and the efforts you are about to make are the key to creating the new life you seek.

As you begin, please know that knowledge of this truth is not enough to change your world. ***New beliefs need to be applied in the physical world in order for them to become transformational tools.*** You have to practice your new beliefs, using them in your daily life, constantly activating them within your energetic body. Each time you choose to do this work you will be creating new outcomes, and energetic resonance will occur. Repeatedly choosing to move from low- to high-frequency states will create energetic shifts that will be noticeable to you and to others. You will indeed begin to experience that, regardless of the chaos that arrives, you are living an extraordinary life.

But for now, you need to start to put action behind your new belief in order for it to be activated. We live in a physical world that calls for action in order for intentions to be realized. Just as you cannot go up to a wall with a hammer and a nail in your hand and tell the nail to magically jump into the wall, you cannot expect the "knowing" of a new belief to translate into new behavior. Aha moments can shift your world briefly, but if you don't choose to do the work of seeing where and how your new truths can be applied and then apply them, they will be nothing more than holy moments that dissipate over time.

This is the reason that I have long had a problem with some of the New Age teachings that espouse "think your way to success" or "dream it and it will come true." While there may be some very highly evolved beings who can manifest at will, most of us need to practice our new beliefs many times before they become integrated into our energetic bodies and our physicality and show up in our world.

In order for you to be able to shift your frequency, making sure to change your state from fear and lack to peace and abundance, you need to be aware of the places in your life where you are now consistently blocking yourself from experiencing an extraordinary life. In this work I will be sharing with you how to become aware of the obstacles you create, then how to use those very obstacles *as your energetic transformational tools.*

We all have blocks that keep us from living an extraordinary life, and as we continue, I will highlight for you blocks, or blind spots, that I see new students consistently struggle with. You might recognize them as well, and when you do, open your arms wide to the actions I offer that you can use as tools to shift your frequency into high-energy mode. Let's get started!

BLIND SPOT

Your Beliefs and Actions Are Not in Alignment

Over many years of teaching I consistently see that the most frequently held block that keeps people from living their values is that their beliefs and their actions are not in alignment. This misalignment happens because we are not only our thoughts, and intellectual knowing is not true experience. Our experiences come from our actions, so our actions need to be in alignment with our beliefs in order for our reality to reflect them.

When your actions are out of alignment with your higher knowing you will always create the results that do not serve, usually fueled by lack and fear.

All too often my students know they have the ability to change their frequencies but they have yet to *apply* this knowledge in their daily lives, so the results they are achieving still represent their past history of pain, not their new beliefs.

Other students do not directly notice their states: instead, they expect that meditation or prayer will carry the load, and they miss the many opportunities they have to integrate their higher frequency beliefs into their lives. Very little change can happen for them, for we are consistently called upon to do the work of witnessing and shifting our energy moment to moment—and daily life is our opportunity to do just that.

But you know better, and you've already begun the process. It's going to take continued effort to review your life and see where you need to shift your frequencies. We worked on that in the last chapter, and now you have insight as to which relationships and situations leave you prone to working from fear. These are the places you can now begin to focus your attention.

It will also be necessary for you to continuously stay present in your life, observing your thoughts and emotions and shifting your frequencies when you notice that you are out of alignment with your intuitive body and fear rears its ugly head. It's important to stay vigilant, witnessing your states as you walk through your day. But your work will pay off for you and for us all, as when you consistently watch your vibration and change into high-frequency mode, you will not continue to add negative vibrations into your world—and ours. ***Your actions will ultimately represent your beliefs and your reality will reflect them.***

The quote below by Swami Sarvagatananda has been on my desk for years as it reminds me that action, not just intention, is needed in order for any energetic shift to occur.

> *It is not your belief, it is your behavior that counts.*
> *It is not your faith but your function that counts.*
> *It is not your conviction but your character that counts.*

Clearly the swami knew that having the intellectual understanding of a truth or intention to act is not enough. We need to put action behind a belief in order for it to have resonance in our physical world.

See if any of these scenarios that speak to holding a belief but not putting the action behind it ring true for you.

- You hold beliefs that being in kindness and generosity are the states you value most, but you find that you rush past homeless people on the corner, hoping they don't ask you for money.

- You "intellectually" know that you are more than your thoughts and emotions, but when you read online posts or watch videos of politicians and their followers who hold very different opinions from you, you give yourself a free pass to call them names and denigrate their beliefs.
- You came home after you'd spent a day battling traffic and listening to your coworkers' concerns. You were tired and exhausted, and one unkind word from your partner sent you over the tipping point, and you snapped back with harsh words and lots of unkind thoughts.
- You hold the view that you need to trust whatever happens, and you believe you are open to flow regardless of what that life brings, but you still shout at drivers on the road or find yourself judging the person who just scooped your subway seat.

If you see yourself in any of these situations you are holding beliefs that are not backed up by your actions.

If you continue to move forward not knowing that your beliefs are out of alignment with your actions and that fear is the leading frequency in your life, you'll begin to feel powerless, and you'll start to blame others for what's happening in your life. The chaos in your life will bleed over into the chaos in the world at large, and suddenly you begin to feel very much out of control.

If you recognize yourself in any of these examples, it's time to align your beliefs *with your actions* so you can change your life!

ACTION

———◆———

The Three-Step Process for Aligning Your Beliefs with Your Actions

In order for you to shift your frequency in the moment, enabling your actions to be in alignment with your beliefs, there are three important steps you will need to consistently take as you move through your day. You will need to:

1. **Observe your actions:** Staying in nonjudgment, be a witness to your state of being 24/7. Whenever you notice you are in a low frequency, go to Step 2.

2. **Request guidance from your highest knowing: How are you blocking your experience of love?** What are you to learn from this disturbance? Be open and willing to hear what shift you need to make in order to activate the frequency of love.

3. **Experience the manifestation of love you need now:** Which physical manifestation of high frequency (love) shall you bring in? Kindness, patience, compassion, gratitude, tolerance, grace, or understanding? Allow yourself to receive and for the answer to land. Close your eyes, relax, and bring into your body and being a memory when you experienced the manifestation of love you now need, or visualize the new vibration. Experience it in your body fully and completely.

The act of observation will provide you with many different transformational moments as you become present to what state you are holding at any moment in time. No matter how deep your spiritual path, most of us spend little time watching our behavior, so this will be a new habit that you will need to cultivate. Whatever your pace, be kind and patient with yourself. It may come easily, or it might take you weeks or months until you get into the practice of consistently remembering that you have taken on the job of watching yourself as you move through your life.

When you are ready to begin, you may want to start by focusing on one state that you have difficulty holding, such as patience. Or you may note a pattern or a predominant low-frequency action such as being frustrated, rude, unkind, angry, or rushed. Each difficult moment or low frequency you may have observed in Step 1 is an opportunity for you to make an adjustment in how you walk in the world in order to truly be holding the energy of love and light.

After you've observed any low-frequency actions or disturbances in your emotional field, your thoughts, or your body, take a moment, take a breath, quiet your mind, open your heart, and ask your higher knowledge: "What is it that I need to shift? What do I need to let go of?"

Some people can easily close their eyes, connect to their higher essence, and ask this question, while others will need to close their eyes and breathe for a bit, allowing their minds to slow down and then allowing the knowing to land.

As you take on this practice, you may notice the answer comes quickly or it may land as if out of nowhere a few days later. The timeline doesn't matter; ask the question and get ready to receive what is delivered.

Finally, how do you know which high frequency of love to bring into physical manifestation? Just as the Kabbalists talk of God having seventy-two different manifestations, your highest frequency materializes in different forms in your physicality. Each of these frequencies is a different manifestation of your intuitive body, your higher frequency in the physical world. You may find that each time you ask this question you are given different manifestations to invoke. Sometimes you are guided to respond with the same state over and over.

As you ask the Universe to deliver the answer to your question, simply open and receive what lands for you. Trust what comes in. As you receive guidance begin to remember a time when you experienced that very state of kindness, compassion, or understanding.

For instance, if you were guided to compassion as the state to invoke, close your eyes and begin to see or remember a time when someone was totally compassionate to you. Recall where you were. See the person standing directly in front of you now. Look deeply into their eyes and as you breathe in, feel the compassion they are directing into you. Feel your heart opening to accept the gift they are offering you. Stay in this state of true energetic remembrance for as long as you need.

If you have never received the state you are asked to invoke, feel free to invite your imagination in and begin to visualize what it feels like. Your imagination is another doorway to experiencing the Oneness that resides within you.

When you are ready, simply bring your consciousness back into your body and back into the room. Immediately notice how you feel. You will most likely be completely shifted out of the low-frequency state that created the need for this practice, and you will now experience peace.

This powerful shift is possible, as memories and visualizations of love, compassion, and kindness are actually frequency experiences that can be accessed and utilized as your response to any low-frequency event. Take the time to actually fill your physical and energetic bodies with the frequency of love you—and the situation—require.

While this may seem simple, as you use it you will feel its incredible and increasing power! I cannot overemphasize the importance of these steps, as they are a major key to achieving peace and abundance regardless of your current circumstances.

Congratulations—you have just transformed a low frequency (fear or chaos) into a state of love and peace!

Having these three steps in your tool bag, and with ongoing practice, you will find yourself in the process of transforming the conditioned, limited beliefs that do not serve you and that have likely been guiding your entire life. You can quickly shift your low frequencies in the present moment, accessing higher frequencies throughout your day. You'll be able to leave your low frequencies behind.

As you repeat this three-step process you will move from a low frequency to a high-frequency state in just moments. I've taken students through this process hundreds of times, and I never tire of noticing their excitement as they realize that they have just shifted their state with their willingness to welcome in the high frequency of love that is seeded in them, always waiting to be acknowledged and activated in their physical world.

Follow this advice closely, and don't get discouraged if you forget. With continued effort this process provides one of the most essential shifts you will experience.

The Three Steps in Practice

When I started this work years ago, I found that waiting was extremely difficult for me. I had lots of energy, and being patient felt like being confined. As I began to observe myself I started by simply noting all of the times that the need for patience showed up. That was it. I just began to pay attention whenever I was asked to wait. I didn't try to change my behavior, for observing was my only task at hand.

Suddenly, or so it seemed, the need to be patient was everywhere. It was almost as if the world were nothing but situations and people that demanded my patience. It was crazy! So much chaos popped up, and I was constantly being challenged to wait.

That's how the Universe works. You begin to observe yourself putting your attention on an area to improve upon, and suddenly you are given lots of opportunities to practice. And practice I did. I used each moment requiring my patience as an opportunity to watch how I was responding.

Once I mastered the art of remembering to watch my state (not just be inside of it) I then began to observe how I *felt* when I was asked to be patient. Was I able to relax, or did I feel restless and irritated? As I continued to observe myself, I looked at the *thoughts* that were created from my state of dis-ease of not being comfortable with being asked to wait.

Before I knew it my experience with each moment of chaos requiring patience completely changed. As I witnessed myself, I no longer focused my attention on each nutty situation, got mad at people, or misplaced my energy by focusing on others. I watched *myself*, and as a result the negative juice in each experience was completely gone.

As I watched the person in front of me in the store struggle to find change when I needed to exit quickly, I noticed myself becoming impatient. I felt it in my body, and I knew this was an opportunity to deepen my process of observation before I moved on to Steps 2 and 3.

I asked myself *Why am I so agitated?* No longer was my focus on the irritation I experienced; my attention was on why I wasn't willing to wait. As soon as that focus shifted, the sense of irritation about the event lessened. Why? Because I had gone from a closed state of judgment and blame to an open state of inquiry about my reason for being disturbed. In addition, I was no longer placing blame on someone else; I was fully accepting the responsibility for my own peace or misery.

I had been lecturing and traveling internationally when I started to use this practice. When my flights were delayed, I started to notice the fear in me creep in, evidenced as my past behavior of criticizing the inefficiency of the airlines and bemoaning how I was being inconvenienced. This behavior was now replaced by witnessing my irritation and observing my state. Each time I became aware of my discomfort, I witnessed my anger for being inconvenienced melt away.

Over time, observation of myself led me to the truth that my lack of patience had everything to do with me personalizing each situation and imposing my expectations on others. *My discomfort didn't actually come from the event itself; it came from my response to it. I was resisting what was happening, and my refusal to accept what was happening created the difficulty I was experiencing.* While I had success shifting my energy simply by observing my state, there was more work to do.

I had learned important truths, but I wasn't always implementing them. I found myself impatient as I wondered, "Why am I so irritated with the world when life doesn't go smoothly?" It was as if I had transferred my irritation from people and events to myself, and I realized I still wasn't at peace.

With each moment of difficulty I knew that I had the choice to completely change my view of each situation, and while I was now successful at that, I still wasn't able to be kind to myself. Instead, I continued to harshly judge myself each time I was negatively, emotionally charged. I needed to find a way to hold the space where judgment of myself didn't exist. But for a while, try as I might, self-criticism kept flooding in. So I stayed present to this uncomfortable truth and just kept observing.

One day after a particularly difficult situation where I wasn't able to stay in kindness, I was extremely frustrated with myself, for once again I realized I had been the one to disturb my own peace. As I sat with the agitation I really let myself fully embrace it, and then I had an amazing aha moment.

I realized that my impatience with myself was at the core of my impatience with the world. I needed to give myself understanding and patience, which are a manifestation of love and abundance. Once again a painful experience, when embraced, presented me with a truth I needed to experience. And I realized I couldn't expect myself to deliver patience and kindness to others if I was unable to gift that to myself.

In that moment of revelation it was almost as if someone had opened up a window in a completely dark room. It was so simple. It was so obvious, but I hadn't been able to fully experience that before. Now it was crystal clear.

I wasn't impatient truly with the woman in the store or with the airlines each time the flight was delayed. I was in discomfort because my response to each of the situations was not of love. I was out of alignment with my natural inheritance, and that's why I was in distress.

All this time I thought it was the cancelled flights or slow people who created my disturbance—and then I realized it was my response to them that caused my suffering.

What I hadn't known then, but do know now, is when I'm in judgment of others, I'm in judgment of myself and I'm out of alignment with my natural state of love. That was the true cause of my distress. Remember, you can't be in a state of love and in self-judgment at the same time.

As I continued to work with the state of observation, I saw that every moment of difficulty was indeed an opportunity to let go of the fear I held, such as the fear of not getting out of the store on time or the fear of not making my flight connection. I also learned another valuable lesson: I realized that bad times aren't isolated incidents; they have a higher-octave purpose.

Your soul generates each piece of difficulty as an opportunity for you to make course corrections and return to love. All difficulties, whether with people, circumstances, or tragic events, are not solely about *what happens*. I learned that getting lost in the emotions or the chaos generated from any low-frequency response distracts me from the work at hand: the job of utilizing each piece of difficulty as a transformational tool. For each event holds the opportunity for us to ask: How am I blocking my experience of love?

Remember, you are in a human form. Habitual patterns may not be easy for you to shift, but with time and energy, patterns do indeed morph into new ways of being, and with your consistent effort and discipline as your mantra, you, too, will be able to invoke the three steps on a regular basis!

An added gift for you is that the Universe has an investment in your spiritual growth, and you will notice seemingly magical moments occur that assist your progress as you begin to make consistent efforts. That is indeed what happened to my student Heidger.

HEIDGER'S STORY
The Aha! Moment

Heidger is a man who had been working hard to become more conscious. He meditated and watched how he walked in the world. While he was making great strides and had begun to make his daily life his practice, he was still having difficulty holding love and kindness when he felt others did not respect him. One day during a conference call, a coworker made a comment that Heidger defined as personally insulting and socially inappropriate. He couldn't let go of this event and was still seething as the next day began. He shared his experience:

> *During my morning run, I began to feel enraged. I completely forgot about not personalizing remarks that other people make, and I immediately went into a low-frequency state and thought about how I would retaliate, how I would yell at my colleague, as I was so angry.*

Then I looked up into the sky as I was running through the forest and I saw the ceiling of the trees and branches and the sun breaking through the forest's roof. I suddenly became present to the absolute beauty of what I was experiencing and a deep sense of peace came over me. I felt the anger, which just a moment ago had been my experience, completely melt away.

This wasn't the result of a thought. In the presence of such sheer beauty, Heidger began to feel relieved and at peace. His anger was replaced by the feeling of Oneness. "I suddenly knew, as if I had been pierced by an arrow," he continued, "that what I should do was to talk to my coworker in a kind manner and bring up the topic without any anger. All of this happened in mere seconds."

Heidger's story is one I have heard many times. The people are different and the triggers vary, but the result is always the same. When you try to observe and take action to revise your responses to low frequencies in your world, the Universe comes along and gently taps you on the shoulder, providing you beautiful aha moments as if to say: Keep going!

As you move through your life using these tools and actions to change your low frequency, your negative thoughts and emotional charges will become an alarm clock to remind you that an extraordinary life is yours for the shifting. No longer will anger, jealousy, and irritation be the landing pads for you to sit within. Now they are alert systems, here to remind you that a shift in your state is needed, and here is your chance to move into the state of loving abundance and Oneness.

Actively choosing to raise your frequency whenever needed will change your life in the most spectacular ways.

You now witness how you experience your world. Your momentary thoughts need not shift you out of peace. The words of others no longer have the power to wound you because you now know how to shift your frequency into one of calm. The cruelty and chaos in our world can now be observed and responded to without taking on the vibrational residue that has long left you in the rut of disbelief and pain.

You are now free to walk through your life experiencing the plentitude of all it has to offer without suffering, as you now have a process that you can employ that enables you—despite whatever happens—to always respond from your highest knowing, your natural inheritance of love!

Knowing that you can shift your frequencies using the actions I've outlined here will be extraordinarily life changing.

Now that you have learned how to align your beliefs with your actions, you are ready to tackle another huge block: expecting others and situations to change before you can experience peace.

4

Live Beyond Your Circumstances

Transformational Goal: *Live in the Field of All Possibilities*

As you continue to use the practice of witnessing how you walk in the world, you will notice that your peace is often interrupted by the behavior of other people, the fluctuation of your finances, or the state of your health and partnership. For beings not on a path of spiritual exploration, it would seem perfectly "normal" that illness or financial instability would create friction, and who doesn't feel that the love of their life would complete them?

But you are a spiritual warrior. You are learning that your well-being does not come from others appreciating you or from your circumstances. You now know that peace is always yours to create, as it is a direct result of your choice to be in high vibration regardless of what's now going on in your world.

Your state of peace truly depends on no one but you.

Please remember that truth as we move forward, because I'm about to share with you one of the most common blocks that people experience to living an extraordinary life: the trap of believing that your circumstances need to change before you experience calm.

BLIND SPOT

You Expect Others and Situations to Change Before You Can Experience Peace

This expectation is also tied in to the age-old pitfall of always wanting more. More time, more money, excellent health, and drum roll please . . . the perfect partner!

Have you ever found yourself thinking:

- I'd be happy if only I was appreciated more.
- My life would be better if my partner was more communicative.
- I'd feel safe and secure if I just had more money.
- If I only had more time in my day I wouldn't feel so stressed.

When you connect your happiness to others and to their choices, you are limiting your resources and not dwelling in the field of all possibilities. When you believe that your happiness is tied to another or to your circumstances, you create a series of beliefs—followed by actions—that distract you and take you further from the peace you seek. The actions I'm referring to are so ingrained in how you walk in your world now that you might not even know that they exist.

Take a moment to review the situations, beliefs, and actions created below and see if you recognize yourself in any of these examples:

- When talking politics or any other subject that you feel strongly about, you need to be right and others need to be wrong. This may show up as needing to continually "correct" others, using logic to repeatedly "prove" your point, or finding yourself deeply irritated when people don't understand that the "truth" that you're sharing should be theirs.
- You often blame and shame others when your life doesn't go well. It's always someone else's fault that your life is not peaceful. Whether it be your ungrateful teenagers, competitive coworkers,

your aloof partner, or noisy neighbors, your lack of peace is always due to someone else's behavior.

- You are continually critical of your partner and always find yourself focusing on the aspects of their personality that "don't work for you." Their habits drive you crazy, or perhaps you feel as if you are doing all the work to keep you both afloat.

- Often you are just plain angry with your life, and you find yourself repeating the words "Why does this always happen to me? I deserve more!"

- Your lack of financial stability leaves you constantly frustrated, and you frequently speak the words "I'll never get ahead!"

- Physical pain is a constant in your life, and depression has settled in because you truly believe that your life will never change.

All of these scenarios make logical sense to the unenlightened. Why wouldn't pain create depression? A distant partner is difficult to live with. Who wouldn't wish for supportive coworkers?

While each of these experiences is real to you, it's your responses to them that need to shift, and placing your focus on the experience of pain over and over does not serve you.

We all have aspects of our life that we wish to change. *The error is not in the recognition of what's not working or in the desire to shift your circumstances but in your constant focus on them as your response to each issue.*

Please remember, we are energetic beings.

We create energy and we project energy. When we put our attention on an area of our life, we create more of what we are putting our attention on. Continually placing your focus on what is not working simply creates more of what you don't want.

Consciousness is like a muscle, and if you want to build your biceps you wouldn't just look at your weak and underdeveloped arms and constantly say, "I wish my arms were stronger." NO! You'd pick up free weights, and with each repetition your muscle would grow stronger. If all you did was focus your energy on complaining about your current physical state and you never picked up the weights, your arms would remain as they were, regardless of your wish.

Intentions are not enough in the physical world. The action we put behind them is what transforms an intention into reality.

Your consciousness responds in a similar way. In order to increase your consciousness you have to put your attention on it and use it. So instead of focusing your attention on *what's not happening* (the lack or chaos you are experiencing) place it instead on the *outcome you desire.*

What I am suggesting you do is to use difficulty in a completely different way than you are used to. No longer are tough times landing pads. You will now be using each moment of distress as an alert system to remind you that it's time to focus your attention on what you wish for.

Place your attention and actions on what you *do* want and watch your life shift over time.

To get you started I'd like to take you through a practice that I call Living Beyond Current Limitations.

ACTION

—◆—

Living Beyond Current Limitations

For our practice together I'm going to use the example of chronic pain as the state to shift. Physical pain is one of the toughest experiences to have on a daily basis. It may seem as if your life is nothing more than the suffering you are now experiencing. It's totally understandable that those who are afflicted by pain might believe there is no other reality, but indeed there is.

Whether you are currently in pain or not, follow along with me, and you will see how the practice works, and then you can apply this practice again with any aspect of your life that you feel is blocking you from happiness.

+ Make sure you have physical privacy and then quiet your body and mind. Close your eyes and breathe deeply.
+ Relax your body as best you can and begin to visualize yourself totally healthy.
+ See each part of your body moving easefully. Imagine you are totally healthy. You breathe with ease, and you move gracefully. Experience this fully for several breaths or minutes.
+ Next, begin to see yourself participating in activities that were denied to you before but can be easily accomplished with your new, healthy body. Take your time and see them one by one. Feel your gratitude for being able to experience this new life.
+ Notice how easily you move through your life, how much you accomplish, and how grateful you are for your healthy body. Feel this completely in every cell of your being.
+ Now begin to see one thing you love to do that was previously out of reach, but in this visualization it's easy as pie!
+ Experience the excitement and gratitude you have for being able to do this beloved action. Take your time here—there is no rush; enjoy these moments.

When you feel complete, bring your awareness back into your body and into the room. Notice how you feel. Check in and notice your level of pain. Are you experiencing more peace now than before you began the practice? Many people come out of this practice feeling calm, excited, and empowered.

Congratulations! In choosing to place your attention on creating a healthy body instead of sitting inside of the pain, you have just replaced your outmoded conditioned response of focusing on what's not working, and you have developed a new response to difficulty: placing your active and full attention on what you desire.

When you take time each day to focus your attention and energy on your yet-to-be-seen-in-the-physical-world healthy body, you are not only avoiding the negative energy you were creating, but you are making yourself more comfortable in the moment and you are actively healing your body, for you are accessing the high vibration within you as you repeat this practice.

This practice can be used for any type of difficulty you feel is now blocking you from living your best life.

Whether you wish for more financial flow, a new romance, or a closer relationship with your family or partner, use this tool to shift the negative vibrations you have been creating for years and begin to actually craft the life you seek!

Earlier in this chapter I shared with you a very important spiritual law: *Your state of peace truly depends on no one but you.*

I asked you to hold on to this truth as we discussed the common block of expecting your life's circumstances to change before you would be able to experience peace in your life.

I'm certain that you're now beginning to understand and accept that your circumstances don't need to change in order for you to experience peace. What needs to shift are your perspective and actions and your responses to any difficulty that arises.

You are the master of your life. You, and only you, get to choose where you put your attention—and you now know that what you put your attention on grows, mightily! That's why putting your attention on what you desire brings about the shifts in your life that you seek.

Viktor Frankl, a Holocaust survivor and celebrated brilliant author of more than thirty books, wrote of these principles. In fact, two of his most famous quotes speak to exactly what I am sharing here with you.

When we are no longer able to change a situation, we are challenged to change ourselves.

Everything can be taken from a man but one thing: the last of the human freedoms—to choose one's attitude in any given set of circumstances, to choose one's own way.

As you move forward observing your state and using the practices I share with you, you will indeed see many changes occur in your life.

You might discover that as each piece of your life begins to shift into a higher frequency, you still want more and more and more. While choosing to live an abundant life is indeed your natural inheritance, if you notice that you are experiencing more *wanting* than *appreciation*, you would be wise to cultivate gratitude as a daily practice.

Always wanting more is a common state that truly blocks your ability to experience peace and is a symptom of experiencing your life through the lower frequency of lack. The antidote to lack is the higher state of gratitude.

When you sit in gratitude for your life and all its treasures—your friends, your home, the food you eat, the air you breathe—you are filled to capacity with a high vibration, and you experience the abundance that is yours, now.

When you begin to experience how much you currently, truly, have to be grateful for, and when you feel gratitude in every cell of your body (not just saying the words or thinking them, but truly *having the experience* of gratitude) then you begin to love what is, regardless of your situation.

If you notice that you indeed continually want more and you sense it is distracting you from a sense of peace, use the practice below daily for one month, and you will notice your state shift into a feeling of ease. The need for having it all will lessen and then cease.

ACTION

✦

Go to Gratitude Meditation

Regardless of your current circumstances there is much goodness in your life. As you begin to consciously note what you are grateful for, you are actually filling your spiritual bank account with the high-frequency energy of gratitude within you that is available to you at any time.

This action can be used at any stage of your awakening, as it provides access to your highest wisdom. In your early days of refocusing your energy, it is particularly helpful when you seek to leave behind the state of always wanting more.

Let's begin.

+ Sit quietly and ease your body and mind.
+ Breathe deeply through your nose for several breaths.
+ Begin to reconnect to what you are grateful for.
+ Review each wonderful quality of your life, one by one, as it arises. Please take your time here. It matters not how many different areas of your life you bring up; what is truly important is your attention to each part of your world that you are grateful for.
+ As you visualize each area, feel your gratitude fully in your body. Breathe into the *experience of grace* that lands. You may feel your body relax and experience your breathing slow down as you hold each piece of your life up to the light of gratitude.
+ To optimize this action, please *remember to observe and be grateful for your own strengths, your talents, and all of your abilities.* Give thanks for your loving heart, for your patience, for your kindness, and for your wisdom.
+ When you feel complete, take in a deep breath, slowly release it, and bring your awareness back to being fully present in your body and surroundings.

This simple action needs no tools other than a quiet spot and your willingness to do the work. It is a really profound practice, for you are giving yourself the opportunity to directly connect with your highest self.

Going to gratitude was my major tool when my life was turned completely upside down two days before closing the sale on my house. This was to be the beginning of my new life.

After fifteen years of being the primary financial source for my two children, working long hours, writing two books, and presenting over a hundred lectures in ten years across North America and Canada, I was now going to only be responsible for myself.

I was going to be able to pay off long-term debt I had knowingly created in order to keep our family home. I would finally be able to save money for my retirement, as I had placed all of my hard-earned money into our daily expenses and had absolutely no savings at all.

But two days before the closing on my house a woman hit my car, and I was left with a traumatic brain injury that found me with only two hours of focus a day. I couldn't work, get on buses or trains, write, lecture, or teach. This situation went on for four years, and I never knew if I'd ever be able to earn a living again.

Clearly this was a difficult situation, but each time I would begin to look at what I didn't have, I would immediately remember what I had been given. I went to gratitude, for I had no broken bones, I had a deep connection to Spirit, and I had landed in a beautiful, quiet apartment with a rooftop garden, which was a perfect place to heal.

For the first two and a half years I continued to go to gratitude for the fact that I was alive and that I had suffered no apparent physical injuries, and I had tremendous faith that kept me out of fear. I opened to the field of all possibilities knowing that I alone could do very little but that in welcoming in the light of the Divine, everything was possible!

All of these facts I reminded myself of over and over again. Each time I did, my state changed. Within a few months, I no longer experienced lack, as I had completely surrendered to my experience, knowing that regardless of the current situation or state I was in, I was being taken care of.

At that point financial miracles appeared that provided an income for me—within the realm of what I was capable of doing—that lasted for the next three and a half years of my recovery.

Gratitude carried me forward, and when I look back I realize it's no exaggeration to say that putting my attention on what I was grateful for throughout the entire experience provided me certainty and grace. Despite having no way to earn an income, being unable to be with people for any length of time, and never knowing when and if my situation would change, I still truly experienced continual abundance. I was more than my circumstance, and I lived inside of that energy!

I share my story with you because living beyond whatever circumstances you now deem as difficult is more than possible! Take an inventory and focus on the aspects of your life that you are grateful for now. If you're like most of my students, you'll be overwhelmed by how much you have to be grateful for!

If there's a part of you that's quietly mumbling in the background, *Easy for her to say*, you might be in resistance, and in the next chapter I'll share with you why resistance is not your enemy; it's your next clue toward shifting your way of walking in the world.

5

What Resists Persists

Transformational Goal: *Move from Resistance to Flow*

As you continue to realign your values and actions and place yourself back into high frequency whenever you notice that you are in fear and not in a neutral state, you will begin to see significant changes in your daily world. Small moments will occur at first, but the subtleties you experience are actually providing and opening a new energetic pathway to peace for you to follow.

Congratulations! You are on your way toward creating dynamic shifts in how you walk through your world.

As you are already keyed into your new habit of watching your Lifestream and observing your *being* ever so closely, you are now ready to transform another lifelong behavior that often keeps many students from learning new lessons, accessing vibrational neutrality, and *experiencing* the extraordinary life they seek.

The habit I refer to is a blind spot that so many fall into continually: being in resistance to what is rather than opening to your natural state of flow.

BLIND SPOT
....

You Live in Resistance Rather than
Your Natural State of Flow

Resistance is defined in the dictionary in simple terms: "Refusal to accept." When I looked into the definition more deeply I was astounded. It said: "Resistance is a measure of the opposition to the current flow in any electrical circuit."

WOW!

You are the electrical circuit we are discussing, and your human habit of opposing what appears that does not initially please is you in resistance to the high-frequency energy currently flowing through you 24/7.

Sit with that, please.

The energy of love is always flowing, waiting to guide you.

When you resist, choosing to push against any difficult event that is occurring, you miss the opportunity to learn the lesson the event is designed to teach you, and you block your high-frequency energy of love. This is why you experience so much pain as you walk through your life.

Remember, I have shared with you that you cannot be in a high and low frequency at the same time. When you are in fear and you resist what is occurring, you experience a low vibration, which displaces your high frequency. The pain you experience is from your disconnection to Source energy.

Please stay with me here, as this trail of events can initially feel complex, but it merits your attention, as it is at the core of your long-term pain.

You may now be interpreting your pain as coming from the situation that you are resisting, but that is a result of your conditioned response. ***In truth, your pain is caused by the interruption of love within your Lifestream. When you resist, you are out of vibrational alignment with your Source energy.***

Take a moment please and feel how monumental this truth is.

For as it is your resistance to the situation that causes your pain, you, and only you, have the opportunity to not resist—and to leave your pain behind.

Feel the power of those words.

Let's see how this might play out in your daily world.

Perhaps you have a doctor's appointment an hour away, and as you get into your car you feel a bit of pressure because you know you've gotten a late start. As you fly out the door, you try to ignore the voice inside your head that reminds you that you are always late.

The ride to your location is pretty smooth, but you notice that you get tense as you watch the clock, realizing you have only a little time to reach your appointment if you are to be on time. As you pull into the parking lot you see no available spots until you get to the top level, and then a spot appears. As you prepare to pull into it, someone comes from the other direction and scoops your spot. Without thinking about it you immediately feel your blood boil, and you curse the driver and feel extremely stressed. You begin to head back down the parking lot ramp and feel panicked as you search for a new spot, keeping your eye on the clock. Your tension builds as you don't see any spots and you are now fifteen minutes late. Finally, a space appears, you slip into it, lock your car and—stressed to the max—you race to your appointment.

But what would have happened if, when your parking space got scooped, instead of sitting inside your anger and watching it grow, you were able to experience your discomfort as an alert system? What if you took several deep breaths as you searched for your spot, reminding yourself that in a parking lot people are always coming and going, and you will certainly find a spot? What would have happened if you had reminded yourself that you are blessed, and that if worse came to worse you would be late and you would just be waiting a bit longer for your appointment? What would have occurred if you had given yourself grace, smiled, and reminded yourself that leaving a bit early would have been helpful?

You always have a choice in your response to any given situation. One of the fundamental principles that I repeatedly share with you in this book is that it doesn't matter *what* type of chaos lands in your life, what matters is *your choice of response to the chaos*, for your next minute is always created from the vibration you are holding. Thus, your sense of peace, of ease, comes from your willingness and ability to transform any chaos into grace.

This truth is really hard for most novices, perhaps even for you to wrap your mind around. You were never informed that you are a multi-dimensional being who has this choice. You were never told that you are constantly directed in your daily life by the high and low frequencies that are within your Lifestream.

You have been deeply conditioned to point to the events in your life as the source of your pain, when truly it is your response to those events that creates your long-term pain or peace. When you choose to not go to fear, to not resist any perceived difficulty, you stay in the high frequency of love and are in flow.

Your refusal to accept what appears happens many times a day, and most likely you never notice all the times you are paddling upstream, pushing against the flow of your life.

Your goal is to relearn how to be in flow, for you now know that allowing all experiences to land without resistance is beneficial; you then are able to learn the lessons that each difficulty is highlighting, and you have yet another opportunity to practice being in vibrational neutrality, which ushers in peace.

As we discovered in chapter 2, vibrational neutrality is a state where your emotional body does not have power over your existence. Your emotions are used as the alert system they were meant to be, announcing that you are out of alignment with your highest knowing.

Unfortunately, most people don't use resistance as an alert system. Instead, they fall into their outdated habit of having an emotional reaction to what is happening and then getting lost in the distraction of their emotions.

Know now that resistance of any kind is an announcement that low frequency is in your system waiting to be neutralized. As always, in order to shift any pattern, you need to first be aware of your state; from there, you will then be able to make the choice to utilize your difficulty as a transformational tool.

There are numerous examples of where resistance shows up in your daily life. Being able to know the places that now trigger your resistant behavior is your first step to transforming what is now a block into an instrument for your personal peace.

Take a look at the situations below and see where you recognize yourself.

- You are waiting on the phone to work out a billing problem. An automated message comes on, and a soothing voice tells you that you are valued and your patience is appreciated. But you've been waiting over an hour, and you feel less than valued, and you just want to scream.
- Your child, once loving and kind and oh so close to you, is now a moody teenager. You feel as if you have lost your relationship, and every time they ask you for a ride or for money you feel that's their only connection to you. You are resentful because they only seem to speak to you when they need something that you can provide.
- You go into a movie theater, and it's practically empty. Right before the movie starts a group of six people comes in and sit in the row directly ahead of you. The tallest person in the group blocks your view, and they loudly talk and laugh. You find yourself really irritated, but instead of getting up and moving to another seat, you sit there quietly fuming.
- You worked hard all day and can't wait to get home to relax. But when you get home, the house is a mess, you have dinner to cook, and, as usual, your partner is sitting in front of the TV. Your partner is not at all helpful and becomes more and more withdrawn. You feel as if you are very alone, and you withhold your love and affection.

While these situations may or may not seem minor, I guarantee you they are not. For each moment of difficulty is a major opportunity for you to remember that low-frequency energy is waiting to be transformed. Your life is full of these moments of pain and inconvenience that speak directly to when you resist what is taking place.

Most people do not believe they have a choice or that they can control their emotions. But you now know better because you've been working on noticing your state and shifting what doesn't serve with the Three-Step Process for Aligning Your Beliefs with Your Actions in chapter 3.

Your job is not to try to stop these experiences of frustration. Your work as a conscious spiritual warrior is to use each piece of resistance as a transformational opportunity to raise your personal vibration and to experience peace, not stress.

You are able to experience peace when you receive each situation as a lesson as to how to be a more loving person to yourself—as well as to others—instead of landing inside of the pain that you create when you resist with a low-frequency response to what is occurring.

We have all heard the phrase "What we resist persists." First coined by the noted psychologist Carl Jung, this key phrase speaks to the truth that I have shared with you in the last chapter: *You are an energy manifester and amplifier, and what you place your attention on grows.* When you resist what's happening, you are actively placing your attention on that which you *don't* want, and in doing so you cement that which you *don't* want into being.

Every time you feel stress it's you placing your attention on what you wish had *not* occurred. It seems perfectly natural to be distressed by your distant partner, loud people in the movie theatre, or your petulant teen. But when you have a negative emotional response it creates low frequency, and if you don't transform it, you lose the opportunity to experience peace. Additionally, when you focus and speak your thoughts about the event, repeating it over and over to yourself and to others, you are grounding the low-frequency energy in your system, long after the experience is over, instead of transforming it.

When life isn't going your way, instead of falling into your old habitual pattern of resistance, transform the frequency. You always have this choice.

While there are many ways to do this, the easiest, most convenient and expedient process relies on a tool that you always have. I'm talking about your breath. Make a promise to yourself to use the practice below the next time you experience hurt or stress, as it will place you back inside the energy of flow, and you will experience vibrational neutrality quickly.

ACTION

✦

Five Minutes to Peace:
Use Your Breath to Bring You Back to Neutrality

You can begin this practice as soon as you become aware that you are experiencing any type of difficulty. When your awareness is activated, safely stop what you are doing.

+ Close your eyes and begin to take long, slow, deep breaths through your nose (keeping your mouth closed).
+ Keep your attention fully on the rise and fall of your chest. Don't worry about your thoughts, as they will be in the background coming and going. Simply let them be, and completely focus on your breath.
+ Give yourself five full minutes of deep breathing through the nose, and then notice your state.

You most likely will be quite surprised to see how calm you feel, as it takes only a short time to change your state from resistance to flow or neutrality. If after five minutes you still do not feel more at ease, simply repeat the process until you do.

The breath has long been defined as the physical manifestation of the soul. I previously shared with you that your first act as energy in form was your first breath as a baby, when your high frequency was breathed out into the world. Your breath will also be your last physical act before you leave the planet. Clearly then, your breath is indeed the high-frequency energy of the Divine within you.

Your breath is a remarkable transformational tool. How wonderful that you have an easy-to-use, always available helper, one that costs you nothing but your willingness to access it, a tool that will never leave your side!

You are your attention, and when you choose to place your attention on your breath, you are choosing to shift the low-frequency energy that was created when you resisted, and you are replacing it with the high vibration of the Divine within you. For that reason, simply taking long, slow, deep, and easeful breaths when you experience any resistance is the quickest, most expedient way to shift out of a negatively emotional state and back into neutrality and peace.

Making the choice to breathe consciously and deeply may sound simple, almost too simple, as you read these words. However, in a moment of resistance, when your emotional body has been activated, it may seem monumental for you to accomplish. But you already know that each step you take to attempt to change your frequency is rewarding in clear and tangible ways. As your egoic body is now quite comfortable being the lead usher directing your moves, you may feel discomfort the first few times you attempt this practice, even though it is the step that truly serves you. You may even experience strong resistance to completing the practice, but don't let that stop you. Keep going!

I often suggest this practice to my students when they first begin to work with me. It is one of the exercises that is universally loved, as it is uber simple, yet crazy effective.

I used this practice just today, when I noticed my peace was hijacked by a sudden painful memory. I was out on my morning walk feeling happy, content, and at peace. It's the beginning of spring now, and the birds are returning, and the leaves are starting to appear. It's that point in spring where the trees are surrounded by an almost invisible glow of color that's created as the leaves begin to emerge. I love this precious, fleeting time, and I was experiencing how grateful I felt. Then, out of nowhere, I remembered a part of my life that is hugely painful.

It was that quick. One minute I was walking, feeling peaceful, and the next minute my mind took me to a painful place, my low-frequency energy entered, and the peace was gone.

Fortunately, I have had many years of experience in observing myself, and I was able to notice that my state had changed. I allowed the feeling of pain to land. I didn't try to push it away. I acknowledged it, but then I chose to transform my state back to peace by breathing in deeply, smelling the green all around me, and feeling joy. With my attention on my breath there was no longer space for my feelings of pain. My transference from peace to pain and then back to peace took maybe a minute.

I'm sharing this with you because you most likely have this experience hundreds of times a day, and if you don't have the tools to notice your pain, allow it to be, and then shift your state to neutrality, your peace is being hijacked continuously by your resistance.

Resistance is always a part of our daily life. At times it takes a back seat for a bit, and then there are times when we are in the throes of continual resistance, and there is so much low-frequency energy in our system that we are completely thrown off our path to peace and we begin to panic.

When this happens we need to leave logic behind and open wide to divine guidance before we are able to go with the flow of what is truly being presented.

PETER'S STORY
Following the Flow

Peter, a conscious man I met through the world of business, shares his experience with the practice of letting go of resistance and going with the flow of what was presented to him.

My solo soul shift from the landlocked prairie city of Winnipeg, Canada, where I'd grown up, gotten married, raised a daughter to adulthood, and developed a thriving business, to Halifax, on Canada's Atlantic coast, became a postdivorce adventure of a lifetime. At fifty-eight, I decided to take the plunge and would be starting life over, hopefully beside the ocean that I'd always loved.

After two weeklong exploratory visits to find a home in Halifax, I had come up empty-handed, and everything hinged on finding a suitable apartment during the last day of my trip. I wasn't having much luck.

I had been dividing my time and attention between juggling telephone meetings with my clients and a laborious search for the perfect living space. I was frustrated, discouraged, and running out of time and energy.

I knew that if I climbed aboard that flight back to Winnipeg the next morning I would never return to Halifax.

I was totally out of sorts and decided to take the advice of my spiritual teacher to stop splitting my attention and to allow myself to be comforted and experience calm. Following her advice, I cancelled the balance of my business calls and apartment viewings and left to take a walk by the ocean to unwind and bring myself back to peace.

When I arrived I began to walk in the direction of the salt water.

I had barely taken a dozen steps when I stopped in the middle of the sidewalk and intuitively turned and looked behind me. I felt directed to keep walking away from the ocean and, with no clear destination, I proceeded to walk. About a block and a half up the street, I spied a For Rent sign swinging contentedly in the autumn breeze outside a red brick house. As I peered inside I saw a tastefully renovated and modern suite. I was impressed and relieved. I'd found my home!

I phoned the number posted on the sign and was immediately informed that the apartment I was interested in was rented, but before I could go into despair, I was told that another place was available.

When I went to see it, I knew I was finally home.

Had it not been for my decision to stop pushing against what was happening and choose to let go of the disappointment and panic I was feeling and to simply go for a walk on the beach to restore my peace, I would have boarded my plane to Winnipeg without having found the spot on the Atlantic Ocean that was just waiting for me to discover it.

Peter's words speak volumes!

He had a desire to find a new home and had put what he thought were the "logical" steps in place in order to make his dream a reality. But because he was splitting his attention between work and responsibilities while he was looking for a new home, he achieved no results. As he got frustrated and disappointed he noticed his fear building and he felt panic (which is a form of resistance) settle in. But instead of pushing even more, he made the choice to change his state.

His act of choosing to use the last few hours he had to find a home to take an ocean walk was not a logical choice; it was an intuitive—and highly beneficial—one.

Peter chose to open to guidance and to actualize his high frequency as his GPS system. That was the opening that he needed in order to lose the distraction that came from pushing against what was occurring.

He was then able to come back to neutrality, which allowed him to be open to the divine guidance that was waiting to direct him to his new home. As he overrode his logical mind and followed the guidance he received, his answer appeared in the form of a For Rent sign.

Peter's story illustrates that we alone do not create our lives.

———————————————

The divine energy that resides within our being, the Oneness of who we are, is a powerful consciousness that exists not only within us but outside of us, surrounding us constantly.

When we push against negative energy that is present we create more of that energy, and there is no room for us to be open to divine intervention.

When we fill our days with activity and work as if we are the only director of our life, we have no space to hear the Divine, which speaks to us 24/7.

When we rely on logic alone, we are using only a fraction of our assets and we miss the intuitive gifts that empower us.

But when we surrender to what is, and we are in flow and we seek to relax to let go of the stress, we are choosing to place ourselves in an open state, and we then are able to hear and see the guidance that surrounds us 24/7. ***Then, and only then, are we are able to accept that we alone do nothing, and it is only in our willingness to be guided that we are divinely led***.

In the daily world, resistance, your conditioned response to difficulty, is certain to be a frequent visitor when you are starting a new venture, embarking on a creative project, or making any significant change in your life that will serve you. Remember the time you created a new exercise plan and were excited to begin? You were filled with enthusiasm. You joined the gym, and you went continuously for the first week and felt great. Then in week two you missed a few days as you chose to let other responsibilities be the priority. Week three found you exercising only once, and then mysteriously, even though you felt guilty, you couldn't seem to "find the time" to work out.

You can replace the example of the gym with your new eating habit, meditation, or starting a new creative project or the book you've always wanted to write. I guarantee you, my friend, resistance will show up in your life. If you find yourself speaking the words "I have no time" or "I can't find the time," these are also clues that resistance is present.

I often hear my students say they don't have the time to meditate or they don't have time to cook healthy foods. Some folks feel they can't become more conscious or connect to their higher essence because they don't have the time to watch their thoughts and actions as they move through their daily lives. Yet the truth is that we all have the same twenty-four hours each day.

While we don't have the same responsibilities, we all get to choose how we use the time that we do have. Time is truly not the issue. Resistance and our choices as to *how we respond to resistance* are what need to be addressed. Your belief that you don't have enough time is actually your resistance tricking you into believing that you have no power. But you do!

Each day when you wake up you have the opportunity to invoke your power by connecting to your intuitive body upon arising.

Use the practice below to reconnect to your intuitive body, thus surrounding your upcoming day in light—and limiting resistance before it appears.

ACTION

———✦———

A Morning Practice: Surround Your Day in Light!

+ When you awake in the morning but before you leave your bed, begin to visualize your day ahead. If you have a commute, start there. See the train, empty. See the roads, clear. See yourself calm, leaving with plenty of time to get to your destination.
+ Then begin to visualize yourself moving through your day, seeing each interaction surrounded by light, with each exchange unfolding easefully and lovingly. See yourself patient, kind, and understanding. See others this way as well. If you have any upcoming meetings that you feel might cause you stress, ask that they unfold with ease and result in the higher good for you and the highest good for all. See yourself open to divine guidance and keeping each commitment you have made to yourself.
+ When you feel complete, express your gratitude and ask to stay in grace as the day unfolds.

So far I've been focusing my teaching in this chapter on resistance, but now let's look at its counterpart, the energy of flow. The dictionary definition of *flow* is revealing: "to proceed smoothly, continuously, and effortlessly."

From a spiritual perspective, you are in flow when you are in full receivership, which translates into you allowing all experiences to come into your life without resistance. *All* is the key word here, for each and every experience, no matter how difficult, has a divine purpose in your life.

Events that you now define as tough often have lessons and practices attached that benefit you. Remember the example of trying to park on the way to a doctor visit? Perhaps the lesson was to learn to leave a bit earlier; and on a higher octave, to give yourself grace or perhaps to practice the art of patience and faith. When you choose to allow an event to land, you won't get lost in the distraction of your emotions and you'll be able to receive whatever lesson or practice you are being given.

When you begin to let each moment unveil without resistance, you are in flow. This is an advanced state, one that will take you time to achieve, but each step you take brings more ease into your life.

ACTION

—◆—

Noting Words and Actions

In order to activate the high frequency of flow as your operating system, begin by paying close attention to your words *and* to your actions. We are energy in form, and we live a physical existence. Your words and your actions represent your focused attention. As we know that what you put your attention on grows stronger, you'll need to make sure that what you say and what you do represent your wishes rather than your disappointment.

All too often my students are unaware of how frequently they complain and disparage what happens in their lives, rather than living in gratitude. The consistency of holding a high frequency, of truly living in the field of all possibilities rather than dwelling on what's *not* occurring, cannot be overstated.

In order to make sure that you are taking actions that enable you to stay in flow should you find yourself speaking (or thinking) thoughts that represent the energy of lack, simply say "Cancel that!" Then view yourself surrounded by light, and place light around the situation or any person that was involved. This seemingly simple practice ends the energetic charge of low-frequency and replaces it with high vibration. When I began this practice years ago, there were many times in a day that I said, "Cancel that!" So be prepared, and keep this phrase in your front pocket, as it will be your constant companion when you start the practice of moving into flow!

Another action to take that will help you move from resistance to flow is to learn how to say the word and be in the energy of yes as often as possible.

Do you know people (perhaps even yourself) who always—almost automatically—say no? No to help. No to new foods, to new adventures. No to support and to the very tools that will create the shift they seek?

These are also the folks who repeatedly brush off compliments, and rarely, if ever, speak well of themselves.

This is a tough spot to be in.

When no is continually your response to help, to support, and to ideas from others, you are also not hearing the divine guidance that surrounds you 24/7. Your ability to manifest *any* type of abundance is completely blocked. Living in this closed state, you are in a constant state of resistance rather than in flow.

In order to make sure you are not unconsciously saying no to life, begin to watch your responses when others offer help, regardless of how small the gift might be. Are you accepting:

- the door that is being held for you?
- the smile from the stranger that you're passing on the street?
- the penny that appeared on the sidewalk in front of you?
- a compliment? Are you fully receiving the words, or do you rush through a thank you and move quickly on to your next thought?

This is a practice of observation, so make sure to gently notice if anything resonates with you and avoid any judgmental response.

After you've observed your way of walking in the world, begin the practice of *YES*. Pick up the penny, place it in your pocket, and thank the Universe for supporting you. Walk through the open door, thanking the person that held it. Smile broadly back at the friendly stranger as you pass.

Then begin to take larger steps. Sign up for the free meditation challenge you thought would be too much effort. Begin the exercise practice you have been promising yourself you would start. Learn new technology that would enable you to participate in social media.

As you take these beginning steps and use the practices I've suggested to leave resistance behind and open yourself up to the high-frequency of flow, you will fill your being with the high-frequency energy that is indeed your natural inheritance. You will then notice new opportunities arrive on your doorstep that speak to the shift you have created. New relationships and a variety of possibilities that you never before could have imagined will appear.

When your attention, your words, and your actions are aligned and consistently represent you in flow, your operating system will be shifted and you will be on your way toward learning how to open to all experiences, whether they are difficult or not. This one major change has everything to do with your ability to keep your spiritual bank account filled to the brim with high frequency, as you will learn in our next chapter!

6

Running on Empty

Transformational Goal: *Fill Your Spiritual Bank Account to the Brim*

You now know that saying yes to all that appears in your life is a key spiritual practice to take on, as it places you in full receptivity and provides you the opportunity to leave fear-based decisions behind as you seek to create your extraordinary life.

While of course I'm not suggesting that you ever place yourself in any type of unsafe situation by saying yes, I am urging you to notice how often you resist and immediately push back difficulty and keep potential at bay. I am also encouraging you to open and receive the many blessings that land in your life.

At first glance, some "blessings" might arrive cloaked in the mask of chaos. These are the life situations and events that others call irritations, difficulties, and tragedies. These "blessings" can involve loved ones, acquaintances, or strangers. Or perhaps a situation lands and you are being given the opportunity to look at your behavior because you responded to a tough moment from a place of fear.

Other gifts might be so small that you miss them: the kind words spoken by a friend that don't completely register as you are rushing too quickly through your life, or the seat that magically appears on the bus when your arms are full and you are bone tired.

Then there is the ultimate gift, the practice of saying yes to the divine guidance that lives within you. Learning how to access and actualize intuitive direction 24/7 is the grand prize you are gifted. It is truly the tool that guides you to the exceptional life you seek to live.

Being open to receiving the many gifts you are being offered every single day is an important shift to make as it places you into radical acceptance and begins to fill your spiritual bank account, which ensures that your Lifestream has a pathway to peace.

Your spiritual bank account (SBA) is the level of high-frequency energy that you hold and retain in any given moment. Ideally, you want to consistently stay in high vibrations as you move through your day. For when you are able to stay connected to the frequency of love that is always accessible to you, you are centered, able to experience peace, and ready to truly manifest the life you seek.

But as you've already discovered, your ability to stay in a high frequency is not consistent because you are saying no to opportunities, connections, and new ideas, choosing only to see the pain in difficulty you perceive and responding with more of the same. When you allow your life events to adversely affect your energetic state, your natural connection to high-frequency energy is continually replaced with low frequencies. This shows up as feeling peaceful one moment and then easily shifting into a state of judgment, irritation, or anger as your moment-to-moment life unfolds.

If you recognize yourself here, you are experiencing one of the most common blind spots to peace: operating from a spiritually depleted bank account.

BLIND SPOT
....
You Operate from a Depleted Spiritual Bank Account

In order to understand what a spiritual bank account is and how you allow your daily events to add to or deplete your balance, let's look at physical bank accounts.

Let's imagine that you're starting a checking account to cover your monthly living expenses. You open your account with the amount of money you feel you'll need for the rest of the month. As the month goes along you write checks or use your debit card, and the money is withdrawn when needed. Throughout the month you're keeping an eye on the amount of money you still have in your account and the payments you still need to make, because you don't want to overdraw your account and go into the red.

Your spiritual bank account works in a similar way.

When you wake up in the morning, if you have had a good sleep and are rested, your spiritual bank account is 100 percent full. Your body has had time to replenish itself without activity. Your mind has been stilled, and during your sleep you were connected to high-frequency energy. All of the different manifestations of who you are have been rested and recharged.

But as you begin your day, if you start thinking of all of the activities ahead and you get overwhelmed, there goes 10 percent of your spiritual bank account. If you're reading the paper or listening to the news while you eat breakfast, and you find yourself getting depressed by world events, there's another 10 percent lost. When you get into your car to start driving to work, and people on the road are less than polite as they drive, you allow their tension to become yours, and there's another 15 percent. If you started late, traffic is bad, and you worry about whether you'll be on time or not, chalk up another 20 percent. When you walk in the door to your office or place of work, as you start your day, you've already used up 55 percent of your high-frequency energy!

If you then start to notice the people in your office who irritate you or remember how unappreciated you feel and then get annoyed at your coworkers, you lose another 30 percent. By the end of the day, before you get in your car to travel back home, you are probably already in the red, your spiritual bank account completely depleted. It's no wonder, then, that when you walk into your home, as much as you'd like to be patient and kind, you simply don't have the energy to do so.

You can take this example and replace any of the components I've laid out for you and put in your specific elements, and you'll be able to see how and where you are currently losing high-frequency energy due to the choices you make as you move through your day.

In addition to the moment-to-moment choices that you make, unforeseen events that carry great impact can deplete your energy reserves as well.

If you run into an emergency—your car breaks down, you have an unexpected doctor's visit, or your house needs a sudden repair—you will need not just more money, but you'll also need to stay in a high vibration. The danger is not only will you overdraw the funds in your financial bank account, but your spiritual bank account will dip into the red as well.

I'm sure you can now see how your daily events, exchanges, and experiences (as well as emergencies) can drain your spiritual bank account.

While many of us have been conditioned to pay attention to our financial bank accounts, rarely have we been introduced to observing and maintaining our spiritual bank accounts. But that all changes for you now.

I invite you to take a moment and review the last week. Note the moments in your life where you went from being in a peaceful state to feeling irritated, angry, or frustrated.

Now, hit the playback button and notice what happened to create this response.

Did someone say something to you that you felt was hurtful? Had someone done something that you felt they should not have? Did you notice a mistake you made that caused a minor issue but felt much larger?

Maybe your irritation popped up when you were trying to get a lot done in a short period of time and you kept getting more frustrated as you realized you were running out of time?

Were you feeling rushed to get dinner on the table and moving so quickly—chopping vegetables so fast and furiously because you hadn't slowed down from the day—that you cut your finger in the process?

There are thousands of opportunities every day for you to lose whatever sense of peace you have and to unconsciously fall into a low-frequency vibration. But you have choice! *You may not have a choice as to what has landed in your world, but you always have a choice as to how you react to what has occurred.* And this, my friend, is where your freedom lies.

Experiencing low frequency is a part of life, but not being conscious of your vibrational levels and always running on empty can lead to depression, poor health, and difficulty in your relationships.

For these reasons, your vibrational health should be as important to you as your mental or physical state. Check in throughout the day, making sure that your SBA is not close to being depleted.

The signs of a drained SBA can include a sense of weariness, lack of energy, irritability, and depression.

I'm sure you've heard others talk of the mind–body connection. I've always found that term a bit misleading. While your thoughts do affect your physical body, it's actually the *vibration* your thoughts carry that affects your Lifestream. In addition to the vibration your words carry, the vibration you hold when you speak your words also has an effect on your state and on your physical health.

Maintaining a high vibration and continually filling your SBA is your key to excellent physical and mental health. Our society in general is just now examining how we physically care for our bodies. It's no surprise, then, that many beings are not aware of their SBA and its importance in our daily health and well-being.

But that stops for you now.

Your first step in the process of keeping your vibration high is to become aware of your vibrational state throughout the day. This is a new process for you and as such you will need to place your attention on your state regularly.

Being aware of how you are breathing is often your first clue to which vibration you are experiencing. Our breath has a natural rhythm that is meant to be slow and easy. The easier our breath, the healthier the body because short, shallow breaths create stress on our physicality.

So many of us have had our normal pattern of breathing unconsciously shifted. Nonstop thinking and continual rushing around are byproducts of our social conditioning to "achieve at all costs," and short, shallow breaths can usually be found in those who live their lives on the run.

Becoming aware of your own breathing will become a good prompt for you as you check in with yourself.

Be patient with yourself as you begin to observe your being and come back to the practice below whenever you notice you were not in awareness of your vibrational level as you move through the day.

In order to become conscious of where your spiritual bank account is, use my daily check-in system below:

ACTION
——◆——
Daily Spiritual Bank Account Check-In

Your spiritual bank account needs continual attention from you, as does your financial bank account. Depending on your spending habits, you might check your financial bank balance daily or weekly. Taking this action keeps you informed and ensures you do not overspend the funds in your account.

As you start to become aware of your vibrational state, I suggest you initially check in on your spiritual bank account three times a day. This may sound a bit excessive, but it's necessary in order to build a conscious awareness of where you are. And it's truly quite quick and easy to manage.

◆ When you wake up in the morning, check your calendar, note your responsibilities, and then set an alarm on your phone or your watch to go off three times during the day. It is helpful to choose one time in the morning, one in the midafternoon, and one in the evening, well before sleep.

+ The practice is quite simple. When your alarm goes off, simply stop, take a breath, and with radical honesty, note your state. Are you calm and peaceful? Is your brain racing? Is there tenseness anywhere in your body? Are you feeling frustration? Are you feeling joy?

+ As you ask yourself these questions, be certain to be in the space of openhearted inquiry rather than judgment. Simply note what you sense and then go back to what you were doing.

The entire practice can take as little as one minute each time you check in. Don't think about what you discover or analyze it. As you begin to use this practice, unless you are in a tither and need to change your state, don't do anything. (We will cover how to change your state in the next chapter.) This practice is all about noticing where you are and practicing observation instead of judgment.

The practice of checking your frequency has many benefits. The first benefit, which cannot be understated in terms of its importance, is the increase in your conscious awareness. Each time you are checking in to notice your state, you are bringing your conscious awareness into the physical world.

Remember how I shared with you that you were given free will upon your first breath and that free will provides you the opportunity to say yes or no to the divinity within you? Remember how we spoke of the truth that you are your attention, and what you put your attention on grows?

When you choose to use your free will to place your attention on your frequency, you are observing your state from the level of your high consciousness, from the Divine within you, and you bring that frequency into the world of physicality. The more you bring your higher consciousness into your physicality, the more your personal vibration increases and over time shifts start to occur.

Clearly, the practice of observing your state will help you later as you learn how to shift your frequencies, and it also has the extraordinary benefit of bringing your higher consciousness into the physical world each time you step into the place of observation.

The second benefit from this practice is more direct. As you observe your state, you are shifted momentarily out of whatever vibration you were in when you chose to take the moment of pause. If you were in an emotionally charged moment, in the fraction of a second that you stopped to check in, the charge was interrupted. That interruption is the doorway that you will walk through when I teach you how to shift your states.

The third benefit comes when you take a review. After a week of checking your frequency three times a day, sit and observe what you discovered. Do you find that you're mostly peaceful and calm, or are you often agitated and anxious? Are there certain times of the day that you seem to be more peaceful? Are there certain relationships or situations that tend to set you off? Or did you actually experience more peace than you remembered? Were you often calm and feeling grateful when you checked in?

Bringing your higher consciousness in to observe your state is an important practice and a key part of your daily spiritual hygiene. As you start this practice, three times a day is plenty, and before long you'll notice that you are checking in throughout the day regularly without even thinking about it. Over time, your observation of yourself and your vibrational frequencies will become continuous and as instinctive as breathing.

I call this "witnessing as you be." It is truly a developed and conscious art, one that enables you to watch yourself as you move through the world.

When you begin to witness how you are as you move in the world, you'll be able to see that actions stemming from fear rob your spiritual bank account.

Make sure to notice which manifestation of fear you often invoke. Do you worry and project fearful outcomes into the future? Are you judgmental of yourself and others in situations? Are you jealous, impatient, intolerant, or unkind?

It's important to know if there are times when it's harder for you to stay in a high frequency. Do you lose your center when you're tired, hungry, or overworked?

Being able to use radical honesty while you kindly observe yourself will enable you to determine where and when you need to take the transformative steps that we will cover in the next chapter.

While I have focused initially on how your spiritual bank account gets depleted, let's take a look at how you can *deposit* energy into your SBA.

Any acts of kindness, generosity, or service that you sit in receipt of, or that you initiate for others, will fill your spiritual bank account. Supporting others, speaking kind words, shining a light on the good qualities that exist within another, noticing your own good qualities, and being grateful for any part of your life all add volumes to your SBA.

When you go into meditation and prayer, read spiritual books that carry high-vibrational content or listen to a podcast where spiritual concepts are discussed, you are raising your vibration. Any act or action that you choose to take that engages your intuitive body, your highest wisdom, will raise your vibration and deposit energy into your spiritual bank account.

As you move through your day having different experiences and exchanges, your vibrational energy levels are decreasing and increasing all the time. With your periodic check-ins you will now become aware (possibly for the very first time) of what your overall energy levels look like. And later on you'll see how your frequencies affect your emotions and your state of ease.

You now know how important it is to keep track of your energetic frequency levels and how your actions can increase or decrease your spiritual bank account levels throughout the day. Now, through Sofia's story, you'll be able to observe the importance of monitoring your frequencies and the benefits of taking small steps as you seek to shift into your new lifestyle of ease.

SOFIA'S STORY
Running on Fumes

My student Sofia came to me many years ago when I lived in Boston and was raising my children. Sofia is a creative professional who has an active creative business and is the married mother of three boys.

When I first met Sofia she was full of energy. She spoke and moved constantly, rarely stopping to take time to breathe. She was incredibly creative and productive and successful by the standards in which our society defines success. She loved her work, was financially abundant, and had a home that other people would envy. Sophia came to see me because she was always anxious and exhausted, and she saw no way to get off the hamster wheel that was her life. She was completely nonstop, addicted to having more than a full plate at all times.

As we started to work together, it was clear that Sofia's spiritual bank account had been running in the red for quite some time. She rarely got a good night's sleep, food was often the last thing she thought of, and she couldn't believe that she could carve out five minutes a day to go to a space of quiet for herself.

Whenever I suggested Sofia take on the Five Minutes to Peace practice (shared with you in chapter 5) there was always a reason not to. She wouldn't be able to do it in the morning because she had to take care of her young sons. She couldn't stop for five minutes in the day because she had a crew to oversee. And she wouldn't be able to do it in the evening because it was family time.

Are you catching the drift here? Sofia was so addicted to moving fast and never stopping that she truly believed that she had no choice and that she could not find five minutes in her day to go to quiet.

While some people might read this story and say what a selfless person Sofia is, always putting others first, as a spiritual teacher I saw a woman who was always racing, filling her day with activities that kept her far removed from her highest knowing and on the brink of a spiritual and physical collapse.

The bright light in the sea of darkness for Sofia was the hour she put aside for our teaching every month. During this time I made a special point of taking Sofia deep into a meditation to release all of the energy that was sitting in her system.

Not surprisingly, each time Sofia came into my home for her teaching, she was rushing, and I noticed that she always had frequent, shallow breaths. Her pattern of breath would change as I directed her into the meditation, and every time Sofia came out she noticed the change in her state immediately. She loved the feeling of calmness, but she was still convinced that she had no time to take on even the practice of Five Minutes to Peace. We went at her pace for the next few visits. Then, about three months into our work, I asked Sofia to observe her breathing pattern and describe it to me. She used the words *fast* and *shallow*. Sofia then mentioned that it was curious that I asked about her breathing, because sometimes she realized she held her breath without even knowing it until she started to feel light-headed. She told me that this situation happened a great deal when she'd be rushing so fast from task to task, never stopping to pause.

Sophia was clearly out of alignment and not aware her spiritual bank account was so overdrawn that she'd forgotten what breathing properly felt like. It was also obvious to me that Sofia clearly felt she did not have a personal choice to spend five minutes a day to shift her state. So we started slowly.

I began the process of introducing Sophia to doing two SBA check-ins a day. Each time her alarm went off, she was instructed to close her eyes and simply breathe slowly. She agreed to this process of quick check-ins and deep breaths for the next four weeks until our next teaching. When Sofia arrived she was excited to share that she had easily followed the instructions, and to her surprise, she noticed how quick and shallow her breaths often were. She told me that she chose to experiment and had started to actively take longer, slower, more easeful breaths. After a month of this practice she noticed that she was more at ease and felt that she was ready to move on to regularly doing the practice of taking Five Minutes to Peace.

Sofia's story is important, as many people (perhaps even you, dear reader) get overwhelmed when they realize how unconsciously they are moving through the world. Even a simple practice like Five Minutes to Peace can seem like too much of an effort.

That's why it's important to remember to take the processes that I'm sharing with you slowly, steadily, and consistently.

Bringing awareness to how we move through the world, and noticing when our spiritual bank account is depleted and when it is full, is a critical step toward creating our peace and wellness. Our breath is the first key to whether we are moving in harmony or from fear.

I urge you to start the easy process that Sofia took on, of placing yourself in observation for a week. Be kind to yourself as you observe your way of walking in the world—watch your breath and notice your emotions and your vibrational state. Are you in neutrality? Is your spiritual bank account usually full or empty?

At the end of the week, should you discover that your bank account is often empty, make the commitment to taking on the practice of Five Minutes to Peace that I shared with you in the last chapter. This first step will ensure that you are bringing quiet and light into your world every day.

I promised that in the next chapter we'd discuss specific ways to change your state, but if, after reviewing your week of SBA check-ins, you should find that you need a huge dose of light and peace, practice the Golden Light Meditation below. This exercise is a remarkable meditation that will fill your spiritual bank account full each time you choose to use it.

ACTION

The Golden Light Meditation

You'll need about five to ten minutes for this practice.

+ Find a quiet room where you will have total privacy. Sit in a comfortable chair or lie down. Begin to breathe through your nose, in long, slow, deep inhales and long, slow, deep exhales.

+ Keep your attention on the rise and fall of your chest, allowing any thoughts to come and go like waves as they come onto the shore.

+ When you feel fully relaxed, begin to visualize a ball of golden light hovering above your crown chakra, over your hairline. See the golden light pour down through the top of your head, and as it does feel all the muscles in your head begin to relax.

+ As the golden light seeps down your neck and over your shoulders, feel them relax as well.

+ As the golden light continues to seep into your body, down your arms, and out to your fingers, you experience deep relaxation.

+ The light continues to move down your torso and your chest and now to your back, and you completely relax.

+ Now the light continues to move down, covering your hips, front and back, your thighs, your knees, and your calves, totally relaxing each part of your body.

+ The light completes its journey over your ankles, into your feet, and out to your toes.

+ Your entire body is filled with golden light. You are completely relaxed.

+ Stay here until you feel ready to come back into the physical world.

The Golden Light Meditation is one of my students' favorite practices, as it always leaves them feeling calm and at peace. It's a wonderful practice to use when you want to quickly bring your state back to neutrality.

Some people would tell you that running on empty, walking in the world with a depleted spiritual bank account tired and irritable and unhappy, is just the way life is. But you know differently! You know that you have a choice as to how you move through your world and ours.

Now that you have an understanding as to how to monitor your spiritual bank account, and you have practices that will deposit positive frequency into your Lifestream, let's take on the work of shifting your frequencies in the moment.

It's time to learn how to transform your negative thoughts, your emotional outbursts, and your worries.

Read on, Beloved, for in the next chapter you will learn how to transform any piece of fear into grace.

7

Use Fear as a Transformational Tool

Transformational Goal: *Transform Fear into Blessings*

I n the previous chapters I've shared with you the places where in the past you have been consistently blocking your peace, your ease, and your abundance. When your actions didn't mirror your values, when you resisted the difficulty that occurred, when you expected life's situations to change before you experienced happiness, and when your spiritual bank account was running in the red, you were always working from fear.

Throughout this book you have been learning how to recognize your past fear-based behaviors. You've been encouraged to use the exercises and meditations provided to release the low-frequency energy you'd created, which had been adversely directing your daily life responses and limiting your possibilities.

Now that you know how to recognize and release the old low frequency of the past, it's time to learn new practices that will enable you to transform fear immediately into love, *as soon as it shows up*. It's time to use any difficulty, 24/7, as the transformational tool it was always meant to be.

Your most prevalent and accessible tool for change is the low-frequency vibration that until now has kept you from the extraordinary life you seek. While you may have previously *unconsciously* chosen fear as your constant companion, you can now *consciously* choose to recognize it in the moment and use it as a transformational tool then and there, thus converting what was once a difficulty into a blessing.

One of the most profound teachings that Spirit shared with me was that the only reason we experience any difficulty in life is so we can remember and experience that we are love. ***They told me that if each time we felt stress or pain and recognized it as an opportunity to fill ourselves with the frequencies of kindness, patience, and gratitude, we would be using difficulty for the reason it was given to us. We would be consciously using it to experience the love that we truly are.***

Sit with that and absorb the words and the high frequency they carry.

When I received that message it ran through me like a bolt of lightning.

I knew in that moment the truth of what was spoken. My life would never be the same. In an instant I became committed to learning how to utilize fear as a tool for transformation, a vehicle that would remind me to be the loving being I was meant to be.

We have all been conditioned to believe that difficulty just happens and that we need to put up with it, or to avoid it at all costs, or use it as a landing pad, or to stuff it deep inside our being. Holding on to those beliefs for years, we have moved forward like good little soldiers, missing completely the true purpose of difficulty. That one misstep has kept us from creating the lives we so deserve.

BLIND SPOT

Living a Fear-Directed Life

For you and for many others, fear has always been an active part of your life. Not knowing that you were directed by it—or that you had any other choice to shift away from your lifelong habit—you've worked very hard at accessing external sources to create the peace you sought.

That twenty-four-day meditation challenge you did, the weeklong workshop with high-profile teachers you attended, or perhaps even the one-on-one relationship with your own teacher were purposeful.

But here you are, still seeking peace.

The good news is that in the moment fear appears, the only person you truly need to engage with in your commitment to transform it into love is yourself. And the only way you can truly experience a shift is if you are present in the moment and choose to transform the frequency of difficulty into love *as soon as it appears*. No meditation challenge or workshop will do that for you.

You are the change you've been seeking. It's well within your power to begin learning how to recognize when fear shows up in your life and then transform it, moving closer to experiencing the peace you seek.

In the process of shifting from fear to love in the moment, it's critical to be able to identify it as it occurs. You most likely experience fear on a daily basis disguised as doubt, worry, anger, and irritation.

The good news, the absolutely splendid news, is that each time you spiral downward you are experiencing your most accessible opportunity—*then and there*—to shift into love. These are not moments to waste. Instead, times of fear are precious jewels to be mined and used as transformational opportunities.

Let's start excavating!

In chapter 6 I shared that the first step in shifting your behavior and using fear (instead of it using you) is to observe yourself as you move through your life. This step is key in order to be able to witness fear as it presents itself.

Fear has many faces, and being able to identify behaviors in the moment that you may now consider "normal" but are actually fear-based is critical.

Fear-based responses may look like procrastination, jealousy, impatience, intolerance, judgment, criticism, unkindness, prejudice, coveting, extravagance, hoarding, or a lack of vulnerability or openness.

In earlier chapters we explored cultivating a new habit until it becomes an ongoing practice: witnessing yourself as you move through the world. As you become the observer of yourself and not just the participant, you will discover that moment to moment you generate a crazy amount of negativity. Watching your behavior as it occurs, you'll notice many judgments arising, tons of self-critical thoughts, many opinions about the behavior of others, and a steady stream of righteousness.

Remember to be gentle with yourself and commit to radical honesty and grace should you be distracted by self-criticism, shame, or guilt. Shame and guilt (also products of fear) only create more negative energy when they become a landing pad for your observation. And believe it or not, they actually distract you from the work of shifting your frequency.

What changes now is what you do with the thoughts and behaviors that you witness.

The simple solution is to observe the fear and have it act as an alert system. In order to do this, you'll need to create a prompt that represents an alarm going off. When I began this practice many years ago, I created a picture in my mind of an old, round, brass alarm clock that had two large bells on either side of the clock face.

Each time I noticed my fear, I visualized the clock with the bells ringing uncontrollably. I actually saw the movement of the bells in my mind's eye as well as heard the bells ringing loudly. It was a visual as well as an auditory reminder.

Feel free to utilize your senses as you create your alert system. Perhaps a certain smell or sound resonates with you more than a visual picture. Spend a bit of time and create your personal alert system now. Allow the first picture, sound, or scent that comes into your mind to be your guide. Take a moment and ground your alert system into your being so that you have it to reference every time fear appears for you.

Having an alarm ready to remind you that fear is present is an important step. But once alerted, you will need tools that will help you to change the actual vibration of fear into the frequency of love.

Tools for Transformation

During the early days of actively observing my state, I was in relationship with a man who was also a spiritual teacher. His work was focused on helping students lose the fear they had. It was then that I learned the phrase that would become one of my most successful and treasured transformational tools: "Wouldn't it be nice?"

Wouldn't It Be Nice?

Four simple words that hold a great deal of power. I began to use these words regularly each time I saw myself in judgment, frustration, or anger. As I shared with you earlier, the fear I experienced often showed up as harsh judgment.

Now with my new mantra at my side, each time my alert system was activated and the bells started ringing, I stopped, took a breath, and repeated the words "Wouldn't it be nice?"

When I felt anger building up when I was exhausted from working so hard and my teenager was once again not being helpful, I found myself saying, "Wouldn't it be nice if he would just help me out a bit more?" When someone cut me off on the road and I felt my blood start to boil, I'd say, "Wouldn't it be nice if that person had chosen to give a little more space as they came into my lane?"

When I accessed and spoke these words, I was in the midst of a really difficult moment. Fear is a closed state; it's a place of limited— or seemingly no—possibilities. Love is an open state; one where we experience expansiveness, the feeling that all possibilities exist in every moment.

You, too, can take on this practice. Take a look at the situations and mantras I've highlighted for you below and note which ones resonate with you.

- *Wouldn't it be nice* if I could release my frustration and ease into accepting what's appearing?
- *Wouldn't it be nice* if I could relax, even though the train is running late?
- *Wouldn't it be nice* if I could lose my jealousy and be happy for my coworker?
- *Wouldn't it be nice* to be supportive and gentle with myself when I see that I'm procrastinating?
- *Wouldn't it be nice* to lose all of the worry I have around my finances?
- *Wouldn't it be nice* to be patient with myself when I see that I'm still not able to trust my higher knowing?
- *Wouldn't it be nice* to fill myself with compassion when I notice that I'm impatient?
- *Wouldn't it be nice* to finally let go of all past slights and irritations I'm still holding on to?
- *Wouldn't it be nice* to see myself as worthy and valuable?
- *Wouldn't it be nice* to be able to speak my truth clearly and with love?
- *Wouldn't it be nice* to let go of the need to shame and blame others and myself?
- *Wouldn't it be nice* to ease into the process of getting older?
- *Wouldn't it be nice* not to need to know my purpose and to simply sit in faith?
- *Wouldn't it be nice* to stop resisting what is and open to the wonder of divine co-creation?
- *Wouldn't it be nice* to lose my expectations and replace them with intentions and actions?

Each time you use these words, end with a new mantra: "*Wouldn't it be nice* if I could move through my life from love instead of fear."

As you say your new mantra, feel each word deeply in your body, and each time you speak this phrase, feel your entire being changing from tight and tense to calm and relaxed. You will be able to physically feel your state changing from one of fear to love in just seconds. This shift will be consistently immediate, extremely present, and powerful.

We've learned that words carry frequency and the tone we wrap our words in also carries vibration. Not surprising then that four words, "Wouldn't it be nice?" wrapped in the energy of love will create such an immediate shift in your state.

As you read these words the low-frequency energy that is guiding your life might begin to cast seeds of doubt. "How can four words truly change my state so quickly?" "I'll never be able to do this." "I have too much anger and pain inside of me to release anything so quickly." If these phrases or any variation of them begin to pop up for you, remember that this is the voice of the low frequency that we are working hard to recognize and replace with the highest knowing within your Lifestream. I'm referring to your intuitive body, and your ability to call upon it as you hear each of these words is your choice. Remember the practice in chapter 2 of pulling the plug from the wall and saying "Cancel that!" each time you see your low frequencies running the show? This is a perfect opportunity to choose to use that practice. Observation and choice are your key building blocks to shifting behaviors that no longer serve you—keep them in your front pocket and use them often!

Years ago, when I started to use these words as a teaching tool for my students, almost every one of them thought I was a little crazy. How could four words move them from anger to peace so quickly? Yet once they actually used the practice, they, too, noticed an immediate and tangible change in their state.

Try it out now. Think of someone in your life whose actions are triggers for your emotions. See them in your mind's eye and remember a recent time within the last few days when they did something that you felt annoyed, irritated, or hurt by. Feel the emotion that you felt at the time, now, deeply in your body.

Now take a breath, exhale, take another, and consciously feel each word in your body as you say, "Wouldn't it be nice if they had been kinder to me. Wouldn't it be nice if they had considered my feelings? Wouldn't it be nice if they could have been more helpful to me?" Notice how you feel now. Is the charge of anger, frustration, and regret lessened or gone? Perhaps you don't feel as pained, or you feel lighter, more open, and more at ease.

If you are new to spiritual practices, you may need to repeat these words a few times, making sure to feel the words deeply in your body, being present to each word as you say it before you notice a profound effect. With consistent, active, and conscious effort, you'll find that in no time your state will change immediately as you say and feel these words fully inside your body.

Isn't It Curious?

It's curious how the low-frequency body, the ego, works. Many students share that the irritation they experience comes from the behavior of other people around them. What they don't realize until they begin these practices is that the low frequency within each of us always seeks to place the blame for our pain on the behavior of another rather than accepting that our negative response has continued the pain. It's not our job to change anyone. Our work is to learn how to respond to any statement or situation from love. For it is our response that creates our next moment. While I clearly am not suggesting that you ever tolerate emotional, verbal, or physical abuse from another, I am advising you to examine and take responsibility for your reply in all situations. For it is here that you can choose love and transform any chaos that has landed.

When I initially placed myself in observation mode and started noticing how often I judged others, I was shocked and embarrassed. I couldn't believe that I was like Judge Judy nonstop. One minute I was critiquing the fashion sense of the woman walking down the street with way too many patterns going on, and in the next second I was busy quietly criticizing a mother scolding her child. Then my scorn was directed at the person in front of me who didn't hold the door as I entered the store, and a few moments later I was complaining to myself about the clerk behind the counter at the supermarket who was way too slow.

I also observed that each time I witnessed myself thinking unkind thoughts about another, I felt defeated. It was exhausting and tiring to see how judgmental I was.

Would I ever be able to lose the critical thoughts that seemed to control my mind?

Then one day I had an aha moment. It seemed as if somewhere in the process of observing my behavior toward others, I had begun to criticize myself quite harshly. While seeking to change my habit of judging other people, I had shifted the focus of my disdain to myself. While I was getting better at noticing my disparaging behavior of others, and I was indeed shifting my energy when I observed my criticisms, I had unknowingly become much more critical of myself. That's how tricky our conditioning can be!

Being able to see my behavior toward others and using it to shift my frequency was helpful. However, the additional judgment of myself was not. As soon as I realized what was happening, I knew I needed to end my nonstop self-criticism.

It was then that three new words became my saving grace. Whenever I noticed myself judging another, I would say to myself, "Isn't it curious?" "Isn't it curious that I'm once again complaining about a stranger?" "Isn't it curious that I've allowed my state of peace to disappear because it's taking me a bit longer to leave the store?" Or a favorite, "Isn't it curious that I'm so hard on myself for being hard on others?"

When I use these words I like to make sure that I'm holding the energy of compassion. The words "Isn't it curious?" are open and questioning, and they successfully keep me from going to despair each time I find myself becoming Judge Judy all over again.

The self-judgment I experienced is only one of many manifestations of fear that you will encounter. Begin to examine where and when you become most irritated in your daily life. Do you find yourself cross when you're driving to work? Are you impatient with certain family members? Do you have a hard time being put on hold while waiting for your call to be answered?

Reflect upon how you feel about the world today. Are you convinced that the world is a colder, harder place than it was when you were younger? Do you feel invisible? Do you feel that kindness is a forgotten courtesy?

Each of these seemingly normal opinions is actually low-frequency energy that is blocking your peace. The great news is that each one is a wonderful opportunity to bring in the phrase "Isn't it curious?"

- *Isn't it curious* that I'm so impatient as I drive to work?
- *Isn't it curious* that I get so irritated with my mother?
- *Isn't it curious* that I feel the world is so unkind?

Each time you invoke these words as a response to the low-frequency energy that appears, make sure to say them in the energy of openness and lightness.

The two phrases that I've shared here, "Isn't it curious?" and "Wouldn't it be nice?", are the quickest, easiest, and most accessible transformational tools that you can keep in your front pocket and pull out whenever you see yourself experiencing fear in any of its forms. I guarantee you that once you start using these phrases when you recognize yourself in fear, you will be transforming your state multiple times each day.

The third way to continue your transformation is to consider what words you use regularly.

Switching Out Your Vocabulary

Our words carry frequency and as we are working to transform from working from ego and lack into abundance and high frequency, replacing words and phrases that carry a lower frequency with high-frequency options enables us to retain our vibrational levels more easefully.

The words we now use refer to the brain and ego. Our new words refer to the higher frequency, to our sensing, and are meant to create a more open and expansive frequency to move within.

Traditional Words and Phrases	High-Frequency Replacements
Good/bad	Serves/does not serve
I/me/mine	My Lifestream
React	Reflect or respond
Goal	Intention
Thinking about	Sensing into
Understand	Aware of
Focused	Present
Proud of	Happy or excited for
Boundaries	Guidelines
Seek or strive	Receive or choose
Work at it	Sit with it
Think about	Intuit or sense
Thinking	Sensing
I think that	I wonder if

I know that my moment-to-moment practice of noticing my low-frequency moments and transforming them as they appear has contributed greatly to the state of peace and calm I experience. With consistent effort you, too, will experience more peace in your life as you use these phrases as transformational tools whenever you find yourself responding to fear with more of the same. You *always* have the option to respond with a higher frequency of love.

Outside of momentary experiences of pain in our life, there are times when we go through long-term personal difficulty or we live in a time of great external strife. During these times we need additional practices to help us transform the low vibrations we create or the low-vibrational world we experience.

As I write, we are living with COVID-19, which has completely changed (at least for now) the way we experience our daily lives. We no longer shake hands, give out hugs freely, or have an active social life. Masks are placed on our faces, hiding our smiles as we leave our homes, and we think twice before even choosing to go out. Many people have lost loved ones, many businesses have gone under, and some people have even lost their lifelong savings and careers.

During this time of COVID-19 fear is running rampant, and those of us on a spiritual path continue to seek ways to stay safe and out of fear. These are indeed truly difficult times, externally. However, you know what we can do in tough times: we transform them!

When times are difficult and I want to effect great change quickly I use the practice of Laying Down the Shield often. It's a profound tool that you can use to let go of a recurring fear or a life habit that you are having a hard time releasing. It can also be used when you are having difficulty letting go of a relationship that no longer serves or you are living through a natural disaster.

ACTION

Laying Down the Shield

You'll need about ten minutes for this practice. Find a quiet spot where you'll have complete privacy. Have in mind a relationship, a lifelong habit, or a specific fear you wish to release.

+ Sit in a meditation pose or lie down, whichever position is most comfortable for you. Close your eyes and begin to breathe through your nose in long, slow, deep inhale and exhale breaths. Allow your body to completely relax, and when you feel ready, engage your imagination.
+ See yourself standing in front of a great ocean. It's a beautiful day, and you are all alone. You feel comfortable and at ease. The

sun is gently caressing your face. You realize your feet are bare, and you wriggle your toes in the warm sand.

+ As you gaze out onto the ocean you take a deep breath and smell the salty sea air. You hear the gulls in the distance as they call to one another, and you feel so relaxed and grateful that you are here at the ocean.

+ Watching the waves come and go, you suddenly notice there's an object floating in the water. Each wave brings this object closer and closer to you. As it lands at your feet you look down and realize that you are staring at a shield that looks like it's from the Knights of the Round Table. You bend down to pick it up, and you observe its shape and color. You reach your hand out and feel the texture of the shield. As you hold it up to your body, you know this shield is yours. It's the habit you are looking to release; it's the relationship you're looking to let go of; it's the fear that's been keeping you from the abundant, extraordinary life you so deserve.

+ As you hold the shield up to your body you realize that it is too small for you; it no longer fits. It has served its purpose and is no longer needed.

+ It's time for the shield to go now and serve another. Standing on the shore on this beautiful, sunny day, you thank the shield for its service, and then you place it back into the water. You watch as each wave takes the shield farther and farther away from you, until you no longer see it in the ocean.

+ You realize that you feel much lighter, full of ease and peace. Take a breath now and allow the air to slowly leave your body.

+ Take another breath in through your nose, long, slow, and easeful, and as the air releases from your body, bring your consciousness back into your body and back into the room.

This is a potent practice, and each time you use it, you are truly laying down and releasing any energy that no longer serves you.

Depending on how much of a charge you've given to any one person, habit, or situation, using this practice multiple times will serve you well.

Noticing your fear and transforming it—in the moment—into the energy of love serves you not only immediately but has long-lasting effects. You are, after all, working with energy. You are truly releasing and shifting your frequency. As you work to release any old low frequencies stored from past actions and continue to pay attention to the energy of love that you now choose to create, you will begin to notice new shifts in how you respond to the very people and situations that you'd felt triggered by in the past. You will begin to notice that the people you felt bothered by before no longer affect you. In addition, your patience will automatically increase, and your compassion and tolerance will be on full display. Your general irritation will lessen, and your own Judge Judy can finally be retired!

When you've been working with these practices for a while and you notice these shifts in your life, you'll be at a place of more ease and comfort. And as major shifts occur in your life, you'll be able to move easefully with the flow of the shifting tides within your life. Losing your old habit of resistance enables all of the unseen possibilities that had always surrounded you to appear.

JANET'S STORY
Choosing Acceptance: Dreams Lost and Found

My friend Janet, a conscious woman who has dedicated her life to empowering others, was in the second year of a graduate school project when she came up with the idea to create a women's center. She visualized this as a men's club for women without the cigars. It took her only twelve months from conception to the actual ribbon-cutting. She credited the smooth and easy process to all of the spiritual work she had done and to the faith that she had built up, which enabled her to get out of her own way and co-create with the Divine. Janet's center opened, and she was thrilled.

But a year and a half later, the economy tanked and she had to close the doors. She was heartbroken. It was a confusing and painful time for her, as she felt she had truly been on a path.

Rather than letting herself become resistant, angry, or critical, Janet shares that she actively chose to be in a state of loving acceptance.

The entire time I was grieving the loss of my center I knew I was still being guided, for I immediately received a job offer from a friend, and I started to work with her. I had decided to give myself time to heal and learn from a loving space, and supporting her in her venture was exactly what was needed. I hadn't fully understood how much I was assisting her and contributing to her business until one day a few years later, she opened her second business. I realized that I had just helped someone else achieve their dream, and I knew it was the time to get back to mine.

Six months later I opened my current business, The Superbwoman Inc. I coach women how to lose the need to be the super woman, the never-stopping, always-putting-others-first woman. I empower women to be the superb woman—the one who takes care of and loves herself as much as she loves and takes care of others. I have never looked back, feeling more blessed, more alive, and more on my path now than ever before.

Janet's story speaks to the trust that we experience when we choose to put our attention on the goodness that surrounds us and when we choose to stay in a high frequency of love even in a time of difficulty. As I shared with you before, we are our attention, and what we put our attention on grows.

Had Janet chosen to experience her grief, sit inside of it, and tell story after story about the pain she was experiencing, she would've had a much different life result. But instead, while experiencing her grief, her choice was to place her attention on the grace she felt surrounded by. When the opportunity arose to support her friend in her business, instead of feeling resentful and wondering why her own business hadn't succeeded and angry that she was being asked to support another, she accepted open-heartedly. Janet continually made conscious decisions that transformed her fears into blessings. The result was that she wasn't lost inside her emotional body; rather, she was present to her experiences, and she was able then to ultimately recognize when it was time to pursue her own dreams.

Having unmet expectations can be one of the biggest hurdles to experiencing peace. There have been times in my life when I had expectations that my wish would be fulfilled because I had been working so diligently toward an intention that I felt clearly guided to. Yet that intention was never realized.

This has been repeated over and over in the lives of my students and possibly yours as well. When our dreams are not realized as we hoped they would be, we always have the choice of landing inside the energy of regret and resistance, which is a manifestation of fear, or choosing acceptance and being open to something better arriving, which is a manifestation of love.

I do know it is not an easy choice to let go of a dream that you have worked hard for. Because of your conditioning, you may automatically throw yourself full tilt into blame and shame and regret. When this happens, pull out all of the tools I have laid out here for you. Be present to your emotions. Activate your alert system, and transform your fear each moment it appears with the words I have shared with you, "Wouldn't it be nice?" and "Isn't it curious?"

You might find yourself several moments in an hour saying, "Isn't it curious that my dream did not come to pass?" or "Wouldn't it be nice if all of my hard work delivered my desire?" or, "Isn't it curious that I'm having such a tough time moving forward?" Or ultimately, "Wouldn't it be nice if I could just let this intention rest?"

Each time you speak these words in response to any pain you are experiencing, know that you are actually moving yourself vibrationally closer to the acceptance of what is truly occurring, and you are energetically walking toward the door that leads you to your next great adventure!

Choosing acceptance is not an intellectual practice; it's a vibrational one. Sitting inside of not knowing why something that you have deeply yearned for has not occurred—and accepting that reality—is a holy practice, one that you can embrace at any point in your life.

After consistently using the practices I have shared with you and placing yourself in high frequency each time you experience the pain and loss of what you have given up, you will be able to finally let go of the dream that was never meant to be. In that moment when you energetically open up fully inside the frequency of love, the Divine within you is activated.

Working with the frequencies of fear and transforming them by responding with love as they appear in your daily life will serve you well, whether you seek to let go of your anxiety or your habit of judgment and criticism or when you are working with a specific relationship, wish, or desire. Each time you use the practices given to you here, you will be lessening the fear inside your being and filling yourself with divine light.

All of this occurs because you choose love instead of fear.

This is the start of placing yourself in receivership, of losing the belief that you and you alone are responsible for your success in life and opening to the energy of the Oneness that is always waiting for you to choose to acknowledge and activate.

All of this occurs because you choose love.

No workshop creates this opportunity.

No teacher holds your hand moment to moment in your life and guides you each step of the way.

You and you alone choose to transform fear into love each time it appears.

In doing so, you give yourself the greatest gift of all: you choose to co-create with the Divine and live an extraordinary life!

Learning how to co-create with the Divine is critical in order for you to begin to learn how to place yourself at the top of your Grace List in full receivership.

Get ready as you are about to take a deep dive into receivership, the holy process of acknowledging, accessing, and actualizing the light of love that is always present within you!

8

Love Thyself: Placing Yourself in Full Receivership

Transformational Goal: *Prepare to Receive*

O n your journey to create your extraordinary life, you've begun to use difficult daily life events as tools to build your conscious awareness. You've learned how to recognize your stress as fear as it appears in the moment, and you now know how to reply to it with a loving response. You've become aware moment to moment of your thoughts and emotions, and you choose to reshape any that don't serve into higher frequencies, increasing your own personal vibration. Certainly you notice that your life has taken on a different tenor.

It's likely you:

- feel more patient as you move through your day,
- receive great pleasure from the small moments that you witness,
- listen more attentively as others speak to you,
- are more comfortable spending time by yourself, choosing to walk in nature or go to quiet,
- experience more gratitude.

Any or all of these shifts represent you growing your vibration, your conscious awareness.

Using your daily life events consistently as higher-octave opportunities engages you in your life in an extraordinary way. No longer are you using difficulty as a landing pad; it is now your launching pad. Stress is now a reminder that you need to give yourself quiet and calm. Any harsh judgment you notice that you have projected—on yourself or others—is now an alert that reminds you to cancel the negative energy your judgment created, shift your frequency, and fill your being with love!

All of the heavy lifting you've done in the previous chapters has readied you to experience one of the most profound gifts in your journey. I am speaking of learning how to place yourself on top of your Grace List and experience being in full receivership.

Full receivership is the experience of consistently tapping into your intuitive body, and choosing life actions, relationships, and decisions that are in alignment with your highest intentions. ***When you reach this part of your unfolding, you will begin to experience a new sense of love and acceptance.***

When you are in full receivership:

- You are open to the guidance that your intuitive body is always sharing with you 24/7.
- You are more easily able to prioritize your own intentions and needs alongside of those that you have long supported.
- You stay present as others speak well of you, allowing the vibration of their words to fully seep into your being.
- You accept help and support from both humans and the Divine.
- You experience the Oneness in you 24/7, knowing with each cell in your body that you are love, and that you are a part of the never-ending grid of high-vibrational energy that surrounds our planet and beyond.

Let me remind you, we are all part of a great collective of high-frequency energy of love that is referred to as Oneness. You entered your body as this vibrational field when you were birthed. As you breathed your first breath of air, you breathed the Oneness into the physical world and your life as energy in form began.

You may think it is the individual personality and history of time shared together that you experience when you look deeply into your lover's eyes, but it is the Oneness that you are truly experiencing. The divine nature in you is recognizing the divine nature (the Oneness) in your lover.

Oneness is what you feel when you hug your dearest friend, and it's what fills your heart as you tuck your children into bed each night. Oneness is what you experience as you sit with your beloved animal companion, stroking their fur, and Oneness is what fills your body as you breathe in the ocean air or feel deep peace as you walk in a mighty pine forest.

It is Oneness that you seek to return to, and it is Oneness that brought you to this book, to learn how to fully experience and become all of who you truly are. ***Being in the experience of Oneness occurs as you place yourself in full receivership.***

I continually witness my students move through the process of redis-covering the Oneness of who they are as they let go of years of societal conditioning that had them responding to chaos with more of the same. In the early days of their work, they learn how to consistently respond to others with kindness, compassion, and tolerance, yet I notice that they usually leave themselves off their own Grace List. Your Grace List is an energetic list of those whom you accept and love unconditionally. Once you place *yourself* here, with each action you take you are opening to full receivership.

Over and over I see my students still unconsciously judging their own actions harshly, filling their days so full of activities that they have little or no time to eat healthfully, get the rest they need, or go to quiet in order to refill their spiritual bank account.

Time after time I hear students share stories about how they're not supported by their loved ones, how they're the ones doing all the work, and how they rarely, if ever, receive any help or thanks for the work they do. Their inability to place themselves in the state of receivership *creates the illusion that no one is there for them.* Often, they are moving through their lives with no support because they have yet to ask for—or be open to—receiving the help and appreciation they so desire.

Students often share that, while they have made great changes in their life and now feel more connected than ever to the divinity of who they are, they are still not completely at peace or fully happy with themselves or their life. Their lack of happiness comes from a lack of peace and their lack of peace comes from not being in full receivership.

Often when I point out that they are ready to put themselves on the top of their own Grace List, giving themselves and others full loving acceptance, I hear a familiar response: "But isn't it selfish to think of myself before I think about others?" There's our conditioning once again.

We have all been trained for years by the phrase "Think of others before thinking of yourself." This is yet another piece of misinformation from the old paradigm that we now get to correct. As we are all a part of the Oneness—the grid of vibrational energy of love—as we grace ourselves, we grace others. There is no us versus them in the net of Oneness.

When Oneness stops being an intellectual exercise and truly becomes our experience, we feel deeply in our being that placing ourselves at the top of our Grace List, putting our own highest good alongside of the highest good of others, is not at all a selfish act. It's us accepting responsibility for our own happiness instead of waiting for others to deliver that—and blaming them when they don't.

Placing yourself at the top of your Grace List, in its essence, is an act of truly experiencing the Oneness of who you are as you act with responsibility, care, and love for your Lifestream. As we hold our own Lifestream in great reverence, we hold all others there as well.

Living in the physical world, our actions need to be representative of our desires in order for them to manifest. When we place ourselves at the top of our Grace List and put actions in place that represent the highest desires that we have—equanimity and abundance—we are walking in our spiritual integrity and we are vibrationally seeded to experience receivership.

Let me be clear. There is a difference between doing *what we want in the moment* and placing ourselves at the top of our Grace List. Momentary wants and desires often stem from our egoic (low-frequency) energy field. But when we place ourselves at the top of our Grace List *we are making decisions for our highest good and the highest good for all, and we, as well as others, benefit from our choices.*

It's easy to get confused when you first get introduced to the concept of choosing for the highest good, and the highest good for all, versus your momentary wants and desires. So let's look at a common occurrence to understand the difference between these two types of choices.

Let's imagine that you decided to put yourself on a new eating plan in order to lose some weight and feel healthier and to honor the body that is the home of your Lifestream. You committed to your plan for a month and created a list of foods that you could and could not eat. You were doing well, and then five days into the plan you were dying for a piece of chocolate cake. It wasn't on your list of foods to eat, but you really wanted the cake! Your desire for the taste of chocolate was real, and it seemed almost impossible not to run out the door, jump into your car, and go get the cake you craved.

Heading out the door to grab the cake is only fulfilling your immediate craving and desire. It's a low-frequency calling, and while eating the cake serves your momentary wish, it puts you out of alignment with your integrity with yourself. Eating the cake isn't just about the cake; it's choosing an action that is in direct conflict with the promise you made to yourself.

Choosing, however, to notice the urge to eat the cake—but not take that action—is a decision for your highest good. Why? Because you committed to yourself to eat only the foods on your approved list, as that would enable you to lose weight, which was your intention. When you keep your word to your Lifestream to take the action that represents following through on your intention, you are acting on behalf of your highest good.

Eating the chocolate cake, a food you committed not to eat, not only sabotages your eating plan and weight loss, but it also creates low frequency because you are not in alignment with your commitment to yourself. While losing weight was the motivation for your new eating plan, and sticking to it is important in order to achieve that goal, being integral with your word is critical as it places you in full receivership and contributes to the peace that you seek.

I'm suggesting a new phrase when you need to make decisions: "May I choose what is best for my highest good and the highest good for all."

This is a beautiful phrase that speaks to not just what you *want* in the moment (your egoic response), but rather places your attention on the choice that represents the decision that is best at your soul level. As we are all connected through the energy of Oneness, when you make a choice for your higher good it is also for the higher good for all.

As you choose to make choices and decisions for your highest good rather than from your immediate wants and needs, you will be actively accessing the field of Oneness moment to moment. This is a holy practice that clearly calls for you to be present to your thoughts, to your emotions, and to the choice you have at hand to further the egoic mind or to choose to place your attention on your highest wisdom, your intuitive body. Can you see how choosing actions that represent your highest good readily shifts you into the practice of receivership? For being in the present moment is the passport to receiving. If you are not truly present to what is and grounded in conscious awareness, then you are not able to truly receive.

Experiencing the present moment is spoken about often in the world of Spirit—and previously in this book—as it is a goal and intention of many spiritual students. It's a state that most people are not in when they come to spiritual teaching, and it's a place that for many is difficult to achieve. We live in a society that contains much visual and auditory overload. Many people live lives where multitasking is as common as breathing. You cannot multitask and be present.

BLIND SPOT
....
Stories We Create

Another common deterrent that may be keeping you from experiencing your present moments is the old conditioned habit of living inside your stories.

While there are many definitions and uses of the word *stories*, I am referring here to your custom of inventing a narrative that you believe and repeat to others each time you feel that you have been disregarded, disrespected, and not seen or heard.

You know that time when you were rushing into a building and the person in front of you didn't hold the door? Did you tell yourself that they were inconsiderate and clueless? How about the evening when you were trying to go to sleep and your neighbor was blasting their music—did you think they were selfish and insensitive?

These are stories that you create. They carry negative energy and usually you'll hold on to that energy long past the event itself. There's no opportunity for you to be in the present moment because you're still holding on to the low frequency of the situation you've created your story around.

I am often asked: How do I stop my crazy mind? How can I stop creating stories and experience the present moment? Certainly being open and practicing the art of making decisions from your highest knowing rather than from your egoic mind will keep you focused on the present moment. But as your life is not always centered around making decisions, having a practice that helps you experience the present regardless of what's happening is gold!

ACTION

———◆———

Choosing to Pause and Observe

While we've been focusing on practices to help you to respond to each situation of low frequency from love, the action below provides you the opportunity to witness your present frequency and state of peace continually as you move through your day. The basic steps below were used in the chapter 6 exercise Daily Spiritual Bank Account Check-In. They are worth revisiting and further developing at this stage of your journey.

The intention of this practice is to bring you back to the conscious state of being the witness of who you are—and your connection to your highest knowing throughout your day—as you live your life. It's likely there are many times you now slip into an unconscious state of walking through your life, caught up in the "doing," unaware of the Oneness within.

Each time you take on this practice, you will be choosing to bring yourself out of the distraction of the physical world for just a few moments to observe your own current state of peace or lack thereof.

Observation always occurs from the highest intelligence of who you are from your intuitive body. For it is the intuitive body that is the witness of the other multiple dimensions of your Lifestream. The added benefit of this practice is that each time you invoke the intuitive body as you are deeply ensconced in the physical world, you bring yourself back into the present moment.

The practice itself takes just a few minutes to do.

+ To start, at the beginning of your day check your calendar and choose three times—ideally a morning, midday, and evening time—when you will be able to do this practice. Then set your alarm on your phone or your watch to go off at these three times.
+ Each time your alarm goes off, immediately stop what you're doing, take a breath, and note your state. Are you peaceful? Are

you stressed? Are you happy? Are you worried and/or depressed? Just notice. All that's being asked of you now is that you simply stop what you are doing and notice your state.

+ Once you've taken this quick evaluation, go back to doing whatever you were doing when your alarm went off.

+ At the end of the day, take a few moments and *observe* what you discovered during your three moments of pause. Judgments are discouraged, so simply notice; your observations are helpful.

Each time you stop during the day, you are ending whatever energetic charge you were in when your alarm went off. You are also choosing to walk into the role of witnessing your Lifestream. In essence you are choosing to become conscious of your present frequency in the moment, three times each day.

This is the beginning of your journey to become more conscious of each and every moment of your life. Take this practice on for one month. At the end of the month, notice whether you have an increased awareness of your state throughout the day regardless of whether your alarm is going off. Do you find yourself listening more deeply as others speak? Are you able to focus more on what is happening as it occurs? Do you find your habit of multitasking starting to feel a bit irritating?

After a month of doing this practice many people note substantial changes to how they move through their day. While this practice alone will not change your state from one of distraction to complete presence, it is indeed a powerful step toward replacing your old habitual pattern of moving through your life without observing your behavior—and your connection to your highest knowing.

This practice may sound quite simple, but it requires that you choose every day to pay attention. Each time you stop, you're bringing in your highest intelligence and replacing any fear that exists. Your egoic body, the low-frequency manifestation of fear within you, has absolutely no desire to be shoved aside. Be on alert because it may work very hard to impede your progress.

Evidence of your egoic body resisting your new desire to be present may look like it is taking a while to actually start this practice. You may have the desire to begin, but you seem to keep forgetting each morning.

If you do jump in right away, you might notice that after a week or so you forget one morning to set your alarms, and before you know it, it's three weeks later and you realize you completely forgot about the practice.

If this happens to you, give yourself grace and just begin again.

In order to place yourself in full receivership, you will also need to be fully present as you accept the kindness and support that other humans offer you.

Take a moment and observe your past responses when your friends and family, or even strangers, offered kind words about you. Did you fluff off their compliments and deflect expressions of appreciation?

Or were you able to truly, fully hear their words, feel them deeply in your body, and completely experience their appreciation?

Or perhaps you gave a quick thank you and then moved on to another topic.

When I began, years ago, to observe my responses to the kind words that others spoke to me, I was shocked. Most often I never let people finish. I would interrupt them halfway through saying, "Thank you, but it's no big deal." I never felt the energy behind their words because I was way too busy interrupting them and dismissing their kindness. Those were my actual words: "It's no big deal."

I had used those words forever.

When someone took the time to share with me something they appreciated about me or they spoke of their gratitude for something I had done, I always interrupted them and responded with, "It's no big deal." In essence what I was saying was: I was no big deal and their gratitude was no big deal.

When I discovered this I was horrified. My unconscious behavior had for years created low-frequency energy that replaced the goodness they sought to create, and clearly I was not in the present moment listening to their words.

I thought I was being humble. But I couldn't have been acting from humility. Modesty is an act of our intuitive body, and I was responding from unconscious actions. I wasn't present; I was interrupting them and deflecting their kindness.

As I reflected on each incident I realized it was the low frequency of fear within me that was responding. I knew I had a choice to make, and knowing that it would not help me to shame and blame myself for past patterns, I chose instead to notice my habitual response starting to form. And as I saw myself wanting to interrupt them, *my internal alarm clock went off* and I spoke a new phrase. I created words that would place me in receivership and honor the kindness that was being offered to me.

My new phrase spoken each time someone spoke kindly to me or thanked me for something that I had done was, *"Thank you so very much, I fully receive your words."*

I've been speaking these words for years now, and each time I do I feel the energy of them grounding me fully in the present moment, and I feel the words of appreciation and kindness in every cell of my body.

Not being fully present when others speak well of us seems to be as common an act as turning down help from others or from the Divine. Our societal emphasis on being independent, combined with our historical denial of continual spiritual guidance, has us feeling as if we walk alone.

Whether you're a woman who was raised to move independently through the world or advised not to need a man or anyone else to support you mentally and physically, or you are a man who has been reared to show his strength by not needing the help and support of the Divine or other human beings, you were given the message that you are all you need, and that walking alone independently in the world is a sign of a strong, mature adult.

While it is certainly advisable and helpful to learn how to accept responsibility for our Lifestream, choosing to be accountable for our own actions—seeing ourselves as independent or separate from those we live among—is a fallacy.

It is also a really lonely way to exist on our planet.

The word *independent* is defined in the dictionary as self-governing, self-ruling, self-determining, autonomous.

I've spoken before about how words and ideas that help can also hurt. While the concept of being independent has helped many people, there are times in their lives when its usefulness turns into a burden, one that needs to be laid down.

I don't believe that the state of living independently was meant to be a lifestyle. I believe it is guidance meant to help us learn how to make our own decisions and accept responsibility for our behavior when we first become comfortable with walking through the world by ourselves.

Independence represents freedom; it represents responsibility; it represents choice. Many aspects of being independent serve us well. But seeing ourselves as independent of one another and of the Divine is where the illusion lies.

As we are all a part of the Oneness, we are not in our world without connection to others, physically or energetically. We are all connected. While you can choose at any time to enact the free will that you were given when you came into your body, your actions still affect those in your local world *and those you will never meet.*

For these reasons I propose you replace the word *independent* with the word *interdependent.*

In the grid of the Oneness we are all truly individual Lifestreams interdependent on one another. In the world of physical form we are as well. We rely on farmers to grow our food. We count on teachers to educate us. We elect leaders of our countries to govern. We need only to look at our current state of ecological disaster to understand what it looks like to work collectively as interdependent beings or not.

Seeing your Lifestream as interdependent speaks to the reality that your energetic and physical forms actually experience. For unless you live completely off the grid and are totally self-sustaining with no outside help or support of any kind, you are always living interdependently. As you take on the practices offered here and learn how to be in the high-frequency energy you were meant to always inhabit, you imbue the net of Oneness with high-frequency energy instead of the negativity you may have previously contributed.

As you see your Lifestream as an interdependent being, and you begin to live the full experience of that new truth, you will find that placing yourself at the top of your Grace List becomes as easy as being fully present when others speak well of you!

Experiencing your Lifestream as an interdependent being offers up another gift as well. For when you choose to actively move yourself into the net of Oneness by working in an interconnected way with all sentient beings, you begin to actively experience the Divine within you and the divine energy that permeates our planet 24/7.

As you walk among nature, you'll notice yourself stopping more often to gaze at the beauty that surrounds you. It's not just sunsets, sunrises, and raging oceans that will call to you now. You stop to look at the decaying leaves in the fall, finding exquisite beauty there. You appreciate the gray days and the quiet comfort that they bring, no longer wishing only for the days of bright sun. You begin to watch the animals in the woods, pausing for long moments to notice their ways of communicating with each other. You stop often to feel the wind on your face and to listen to the cry of the hoot owl in the distance.

Experiencing the interdependence of all, you'll notice that you sense the energy of the people around you more easily. You'll find yourself listening more deeply as others speak to you, and you'll feel an urgency as you experience your need to serve others. The Divine in you is flowing as you move through the world gracing others with your newfound experience of the Oneness!

As you continue to experience the world around you through the gift of increased awareness and connection, you begin to fully open to receive the divine guidance that is waiting to support you! At this point of your journey you will continue to experience the Divine within you through many daily experiences. In order to help you to deepen your ability to receive the frequency of love in its many forms, the practice Open to Receive is offered to you below.

ACTION

———◆———

Guided Meditation—Open to Receive

Before you begin this meditation, make sure you will have quiet and privacy for at least fifteen minutes. Choose a person who has loved you unconditionally in this lifetime. It matters not whether they are still on the planet or have transitioned off. This will be the person that you bring into the following meditation.

+ Place yourself in a position where you are entirely relaxed, whether you are sitting upright or lying down.
+ Close your eyes and begin taking long, slow, deep breaths in and out of your nose. Create a pattern of breath as you continue to breathe this way.
+ Experience all of the muscles in your body—from the top of your head down through the back of your neck, throughout the torso, out your arms and fingers, your hips, your legs, and out to your toes—becoming completely relaxed.
+ Continue the regular breaths, feeling your being receding more deeply into quiet and peace.
+ Invoke your imagination and see yourself standing in the midst of a great pine forest. It's a beautiful, sunny day, and as you begin to walk in the forest, you feel the sun making its way through the tops of the pine trees and resting on your cheek and your shoulders. You feel safe and comfortable and oh so relaxed.
+ Take a deep breath and as you continue to slowly walk the path, smell the scent of pine. The forest is quiet and you hear the dry pine needles of years past crunch beneath your feet.

+ You come to a place where the path stops, and you notice that it splits in two. As you look to see whether you will take the left or the right path, you notice someone walking toward you on the path to the right.
+ As they get closer you recognize that this is the being that has unconditionally loved you and your life.
+ Soon they are standing in front of you.
+ You are so excited to see them, and you immediately look deeply into each other's eyes.
+ As you stand there looking into their eyes, you feel the love and acceptance they have for you, fully and completely in a way you have never experienced before.
+ They open their arms wide, and you rest your head on their chest as they close their arms around you. You not only hear, but you feel their heartbeat in sync with yours.
+ You feel yourself completely opening; you know you are seen, completely known and totally loved.
+ With every breath you take, drink in this energy fully and completely, with every cell of your body.
+ When you are finished receiving the gift of this loving energy, they release their arms.
+ You step back, and you once again look deeply into each other's eyes, and without any words spoken you thank each other.
+ Your chosen being turns and walks back into the ether.
+ Take several long slow breaths in and out, bringing your consciousness back into your body and back into the room.

Notice how you feel as you come out of this meditation and back into the room. I can't do this practice without feeling incredibly filled and vibrationally shifted, and every student I have taken through this practice is visibly moved, many sharing that this is the most profound spiritual experience they have ever had.

As you practice this meditation, you are actually filling yourself with the vibration of love, through the experience of the vibration of the being whom you choose to bring into the practice.

The practice I have just shared with you will indeed fill you with a high vibration as you open to receiving divine love and love from another.

As you move through the world, continuing to open to full receivership, you will witness how extraordinary divine guidance truly is! At first you may just simply notice that subtle connections in your physical world start to occur. Perhaps you were thinking of someone, and the next minute your computer beeps to tell you that you have an email, and lo and behold it's from the person you were just thinking of. Maybe you noticed that you needed a stand for one of your large house plants, and on your walk that afternoon, a beautiful carved wooden stand that was exactly what you're looking for appears on the side of the road. These experiences and many more have happened to me and to my students, and I'm certain that you can add your own stories.

These episodes that many would call synchronicity are actually examples of the Divine guiding you in your life. High-frequency guidance shows up in different ways. While many are used to going to prayer and asking directly for help, others keep their eyes, ears, and consciousness open 24/7, allowing the Divine to be heard consistently.

My experience is that the Divine—our intuitive body—is always guiding us, but we are rarely listening. Cultural, religious, and societal conditioning may be the reason for your past inability to communicate with the Divine, but this holy communication becomes available now as you place yourself in receivership.

You don't need to be a monk, a nun, a rabbi, or a guru in the mountains of Nepal to receive divine guidance, but you do need to be present in order to hear the guidance as it arrives.

In my earlier days as a student, I rarely asked the Divine for anything and seldom sat and spoke directly to specific masters like Buddha, Maitreya, or Mother Mary. I worked diligently to maintain my integrity. I meditated often, and I walked in my physical world as the witness, not only as the doer. My senses of sight and sound had long been on alert, and I had added in my intuitive body. My "sensing" self was continually activated. I worked hard to lose my habit of creating stories when I felt pain, and I ultimately became grounded in the present moment.

As I moved through my days I heard Spirit's guidance often. Spiritual direction, for me, doesn't show up as a thought; it feels like a "knowing," which feels different than a thought. When I am thinking, my brain is focused on a specific topic. I know what it feels like to have a problem and try to solve that.

For me, a *knowing* simply lands in my field. It often comes when I'm not even focused on the topic that the guidance pertains to, and often it comes through as a complete concept.

Divine direction often lands for me when I am in the midst of cooking or cleaning or engaged in a solo activity.

In 2012 I was cooking dinner for my boys, and I remember so clearly that I had been moving from the counter to the refrigerator when I internally heard the words "It's time to sell the house." I was preparing a meal, and the last thing I was thinking of was whether I should move. While in previous years I had often thought to myself that I would sell my house once the boys were grown, and indeed my boys were at the time young adults, selling our home was the furthest thing from my mind when Spirit came through with that direction.

The words that Spirit spoke were loud and clear. As soon as dinner was over I sat down and engaged my brain and examined my world. The real estate market had turned around, my boys were well beyond high school, and they were both in committed relationships and about to move in with their girlfriends. My business plan had worked well, and my spiritual teaching community was growing. It was indeed time to sell our homestead and have each of us start our new lives.

While receiving spiritual direction is a common occurrence for me, others have had different experiences. A former student, Sam, experienced his guidance as an aha moment while he was in the midst of a time of great loss and pain.

SAM'S STORY
The Gift of Receivership

Sam, a devoted student of consciousness, had thrown his back out helping a neighbor move a TV. His physical body was still hurting quite a bit when his sister arrived for a weeklong visit. As they shared time together, Sam witnessed firsthand how difficult her daily life was. She was a working, single mother with a child who needed a great deal of care, and as Sam realized that his sister was completely exhausted, his heart hurt for her. A few days into his sister's visit, Sam learned that a good friend of his had passed away quite suddenly.

The loss of Sam's friend combined with his concern for his sister—all while he was in constant physical pain—challenged all of his experienced wisdom. He became deeply sad and depressed and couldn't fully express or move through what was happening. For the first time in many years Sam found himself unable to shift his state. His focus was completely on the loss he was experiencing, until Spirit delivered to him yet another opportunity to shift his attention.

Sam shares:

By the time I heard the news of my friend's passing I was feeling beat up physically, emotionally, and even spiritually. Fortunately, that Saturday evening there was a gathering of the spiritual group that I'm involved with. I had not originally intended to go to the event as I was in no mood to socialize, and my sister was visiting. However, my intuitive body spoke loudly and consistently, encouraging me to go. I hesitated, but at the last moment I followed my higher knowing and I went.

During the evening, I received tremendous love and support from everyone there, and their unconditional acceptance set the stage for a huge aha moment for me. I suddenly realized why my friend's death had hit me so hard. His death happened much in the same way as my dad's death many years before. My father had died suddenly during another visit from my sister. As I remembered this, I realized that the pain that I thought I was experiencing around my friend's death was actually also about my father's passing. Then my aha moment happened as I realized that both of these losses represented my fear of losing all the people in my life who cared about me.

As this awareness set in, I looked around the room and saw the many people whom I was connected to and who supported and loved me. I realized that while another person had indeed left my life, love and connection are always available to me.

After the event was over I realized that choosing to listen to my divine direction to attend the event was a gift that delivered not only the support I needed at the time, but also presented to me an understanding of a deeper issue that was healed as I became aware of its presence.

Sam's story is deeply profound. We are energy living in form in a physical world. While there are always physical world reasons when difficulties arise, there are also higher-octave opportunities as well. I've been sharing with you all along how difficulty always has a higher purpose, to give you an opportunity to respond with love.

Sam originally resisted attending the event during a difficult week but heeded his higher guidance and placed himself in receivership. Never did he imagine that by following the guidance he received to attend the gathering that he would come to a profound understanding that would open his heart even more. *That, my friend, is what divine guidance delivers: unexpected gifts when you least expect them.*

When you choose to place yourself in full receivership, you become present in the moment, fully integrating kindness and help from others. In doing so, you open the channel to divine guidance. You begin to hear your intuitive body speak to you clearly. You realize that you do not walk alone in your world. You begin to see yourself as interdependent, realizing that as you live in and emanate the frequencies of love, help, and support, the cycle comes back to you not only from other humans but also from the field of the Oneness, the higher intelligence that lives within you and created us all.

As this understanding becomes your experience and not just an intellectual thought, the vast beauty of the world unfolds in front and inside of you. Your world has changed. Never again will you be without Divine guidance. You are now truly interdependent, open and listening and guided by the Divine within you and within us all.

Your work now is to begin to integrate everything you have learned, taking actions that represent your new state of interconnectedness to the Oneness and love that surrounds you as you continue placing yourself in receivership. This indeed is your next step as you activate your new guided lifestyle, one that is rooted in consciousness and love.

9

Activate Your New Lifestyle!

Transformational Goal:
Integrating What You Have Learned into Your Daily Life

As you have now learned how to use daily difficulties as alerts, responding to them from the higher frequencies of kindness and compassion, and as you open to your intuitive body's guidance—living in an interdependent way and welcoming the support that exists around you 24/7—you will begin to experience your life as nothing short of extraordinary!

You may have heard the expression describing life as "It's not the destination, it's the journey." The wisdom in this statement is profound. For the extraordinary life you create is indeed experienced as a verb, not a noun. There is not only one destination. There is only the ongoing work and the exceptional results of your efforts.

When you continue to witness your being as you walk through your daily life, aware of your actions and choosing to reset your vibration when low frequency is present, you will no longer be creating the negative energy you generated before, when you responded from fear. Your personal energy field will remain clear as you continually release external low frequencies that come and go, and you will begin to experience a level of sustaining peace.

As you consistently place yourself on the top of your own Grace List and receive from the Divine as well as from other humans, you continue to seamlessly move from difficulty into peace, and the questions you ask quickly find solutions—or dissipate completely.

Your vibration attracts like energy, and as you hold yourself and others in grace you will notice that you bring to yourself experiences and relationships that match your newfound higher vibration.

All of your efforts are not just creating changes in your life; you are in essence creating a completely new lifestyle, one that will deliver more of the peace and equanimity that you seek. Your new lifestyle of living an extraordinary life will deliver much to your doorstep, yet you have just begun your journey.

Your life will not be pain free, and inconvenience will not completely disappear. You live on a planet that is filled with paradox and alive with a variety of vibrational forces, and you still have many years of societal conditioning to release and replace with a higher vibration.

Your work is, indeed, ongoing.

Moving through the world consistently tapped into your intuitive body will bring daily experiences that meet you at the level of consciousness where you currently reside. Some of these experiences will carry difficulty in order for you to continually release old patterns and open to your new way of responding from love.

Often, as students move into this more advanced level of growth, they are surprised when they see themselves facing situations they experienced before and thought they were done with. I'm often asked, "Why am I still repeating these same mistakes? Doesn't Spirit know that I've been working on this part of my life? Is Spirit just testing me?" I don't believe that Spirit ever tests us; rather we are given opportunities to practice that which we need to shift in order to become more loving and accepting.

Louise, a devoted student who has worked with me for years, noticed that she was continually working with the harsh judgment she often felt for others. As she continued her work and became more tolerant and loving, her focus then shifted to the judgment she held of herself. The Divine provided her with many opportunities to make mistakes in order for her to be able to kindly take responsibility and give herself loving acceptance. To her credit, Louise embraced each situation as an opportunity to practice the acceptance she had up until then longed to experience.

Stefan, another long-term student, originally came to see me as he sought peace and quiet. But he filled his schedule with so many tasks and social plans that he never had a moment of downtime. His brain never stopped chattering, and he found that peace was not even a possibility because he couldn't quiet his mind.

After taking on the initial practices I provided and building his awareness, Stefan began to prioritize and schedule out quiet time during each day. As Stefan built in time for his inner work, he found more interesting and exciting opportunities appearing in his daily life. He wondered if Spirit was testing him by offering him exciting distractions to keep him from meditating and simply sitting in quiet.

I shared with him, and I share with you now, that the Divine never tests us; it simply provides opportunities for us to practice what is truly beneficial for our higher good.

Vibrational growth does not run in a linear pattern; it runs in a continually upward, circular motion. Our energy continues to spiral up each time we choose to take actions that move us in the direction of our highest good.

While at times it may have looked to both Louise and Stefan that the Divine was testing them, what was truly happening was that they were being given continual opportunities in the physical world to practice their new pattern of prioritizing their spiritual growth over past behavior and physical world distractions.

We each have areas in our lives that are specific to us, that contain our opportunities for growth. These aspects are witnessed through situations that present themselves over and over, providing us opportunities to practice the energetic shifts we need to make in order to release old low-frequency vibrations and build onto our new high-frequency core.

If you are practicing patience, each time you choose to notice your stress being delayed and you choose to end the charge of impatience by taking a breath and filling yourself with gratitude, you increase your high vibration. Because you have experienced years of conditioned responses that have layered the frequency of fear deeply within your being, you have much energy to shift, so you will be presented with many opportunities to practice the high frequency of letting go of expectations of yourself and of others. That is why similar situations will occur even after you feel your shifts had already been accomplished. Clearly, there is additional low frequency to transform.

Should you see yourself feeling as if you take one step forward and three steps back, stop. Take a deep breath and remind yourself, "There are no steps back. Here too, is an opportunity for me to be patient and loving with myself."

The beauty of this work is that each step of the way, even your need to be patient with yourself and the process is a moment to practice that which you need to release.

Having patience with the process of letting go of your expectations, timelines, and impatience is another opportunity to do the transformational work needed in order for you to become a more conscious being.

Sit with that for a moment and feel the power here. For even when you missed the opportunity to practice patience with others, if you do not go to guilt and recrimination and instead you give yourself grace, you have then used that moment to transform the energy, and the teaching is not lost—your frequency has risen.

If you are working on holding more kindness for others and you continue to move through times when you see you weren't kind, acknowledge your missed opportunity, and be kind to yourself when you couldn't be kind to others. For then you still sit inside of the energy of kindness.

Are you sensing here how your transformation is achieved? Opportunities abound for you to continuously place yourself in a higher vibration regardless of what appears.

You now know that we are all connected through Oneness, and your opportunity to shift into a higher vibration is experienced when you transform your reaction to chaos to a loving response, whether it involves another being or simply yourself. If you notice that you've been out of alignment with the frequency of love, and you missed an opportunity to transform through a particular experience, you always have the opening to acknowledge to yourself your missed step and then to give yourself grace, thus creating in the present moment the neutral energy you missed the first time around.

So much of your past conditioning (that you are releasing daily) positions all difficulty as loss and all loss as difficulty.

But you now have the intellectual understanding, and through the teachings, tools, and practices you've used in this book to date, you know that any loss or difficulty is an opportunity to experience the frequency of love and increase your consciousness.

While you will continue to have experiences to live this knowledge through daily events, major shifts in your life—the loss of good health, a relationship, a treasured job, or a beloved being—will most likely still be experienced through grief and lack.

These, once again, are conditioned responses and areas where even the most seasoned student feels challenged.

When one of our beloveds transitions off planet, of course we will miss their physical presence. That is, if we don't believe that they have an energetic body and we don't choose to experience their essence.

Losing your current job, receiving a diagnosis of an illness, or experiencing an accident where you are injured can bring fear charging back into your life. It is here that your graduate work begins, as you are being asked under an extreme situation to retain the vibration you've worked so hard to develop and maintain. While the practices shared with you in this book help you to greatly maintain your vibration, I offer the practice below as it will help you to experience any loss from the energy of love, keeping fear at bay.

The practice below will provide you with an energetic opportunity to change any current or past experience of loss into the energy of love.

ACTION

———✦———

Experiencing Loss through Love

Before you begin this meditation, make sure you will have quiet and privacy for at least fifteen minutes.

While this practice can be utilized for any job, health, or financial loss that you have sustained, for the sake of this example we will be practicing with the loss of a loved one.

+ Place yourself in a position where you are comfortable sitting or lying down. Close your eyes and begin long, slow, deep in-and-out breaths through your nose. Create a regular pattern of breath as you continue to breathe this way.
+ Experience all of the muscles in your body—from the top of your head down through the back of your neck, to the torso of your body, then out to your arms and fingers, your hips, your legs, and out to your toes—becoming completely relaxed.
+ Continue to breathe deeply, feeling your being receding more deeply into quiet and peace.
+ When you feel completely relaxed, begin to visualize the beloved being who has left the earth or with whom you are no longer in a relationship.
+ See them clearly and as you do, begin to visualize their many wonderful qualities. Slowly see each aspect of your beloved, one by one, making sure to feel each one deeply inside your body and energy system. There is no rush here; take your time.

+ Then begin to remember an experience that you had with this person where they fully supported you, a time when their love and support was clearly felt and moved you deeply. Visualize the exact spot where this experience took place; notice who was there, making sure to see all of the details. Remember exactly what happened that touched you so. Feel the experience of this moment fully in your body and in your energy field.

+ Now remember another experience with this beloved being where you totally supported them. Once again remember all of the details of where you were, who was with you, and what transpired. Experience the total love and complete appreciation you had for them. Feel all of this deeply in your being and stay here for as long as you choose.

+ When you're ready to come out of the practice thank them for their unwavering love and support and thank them for receiving your unconditional love for them. Take several breaths back in and out of your body and slowly and easefully bring yourself back into your body and into the room.

As you reenter the room notice how you feel. Most people report feeling emotional, filled with love and gratitude, for they have experienced their beloved's frequency as if they were right there. Experiencing the energy field of our loved ones is the beauty of this practice. Their body may expire but their energy never does and can be called upon whenever you wish.

When I was recovering from my brain injury and still severely impaired, I was asked to share this practice with an audience of high-ranking female military officers (admirals and generals) and top business CEO and CFOs who were retiring. Instead of focusing on a person they had lost, I asked them to use the careers they had just left as their focus for the meditation.

These were powerful women whose entire lifetimes had been

devoted to leading others in the military or in major corporations. Their identities had been formed around the jobs they had held for years.

While I was honored to be invited to teach, I was uncertain how the meditation would be received. I had no idea if any of these women had any connection to Spirit or what that connection might look like. In addition, my brain injury had left me with two and a half hours a day where I could communicate with others and try to focus my thoughts. I would have to rest all day in order to be able to lead the women through a twenty-minute practice.

Not sure if I was physically capable of doing so, I accepted the invitation because when Spirit gives me the opportunity to teach, I know that they know what I am truly capable of.

Any fear I had that my brain would not be capable of performing the teaching needed to be released. Any anxiety I experienced around sharing such highly evolved spiritual information with an audience so grounded in the physical world needed to be vanquished.

I happily accepted the invitation. I led the group of thirty women through a variation of the practice I just shared with you. At the end of the meditation, there was not a dry eye in the house.

Many of the women came up to me after the practice to thank me for helping them to experience the loss of their careers and their lifestyle through joy. One woman shared that she had felt so empty and lost because the military was the only family she knew. Through the practice, she realized how much she had created and how many people she had supported, and she now felt filled to the brim with gratitude for all that she had created and for those she had helped. She shared that she now felt excited to see what her new life would reveal.

As you continue to learn to experience what you have been trained to see as a loss through the eyes of love, you will have new tools and a new perspective to access should you experience the loss of your health, your job, or a relationship.

Relationships are an important aspect of our life, and they add to the pleasure and richness that we all seek. They also offer us the opportunity to continue to move forward with the work of living in high frequency.

Few relationships consistently run smoothly, and when you notice a relationship hitting a rocky patch, instead of becoming defensive, angry, or hurt as you might have in the past before you picked up this book, go to quiet. Look at your behavior and ask your higher knowing, "How did I contribute to the situation and what am I to learn?"

As you receive guidance, make sure to listen with an open heart, and as you notice your own piece in the disturbance, acknowledge it, communicate, and thank your new lifestyle of awareness for helping you to continue to evolve as a conscious being through this relationship.

If the answer doesn't land immediately, keep your eyes and ears and sensing wide open for the message that will be delivered. As you hear the words or receive a sense or feel a knowing that speaks to the actions you are to take, know that your new lifestyle is delivering here as well.

As you well know, relationships with friends, lovers, and sometimes even with families may need a pause or even call for a complete break. Letting go of relationships that no longer truly serve you is rarely easy. In fact, for most people, unless you have experienced physical or emotional abuse, it's usually quite difficult to let go of relationships when they no longer serve.

When relationships should be released, people often stay in them far longer than they know they should. It's not just the years and the memories; it's truly the energetic ties they have with others that keep them held in place. Not surprisingly, some of that energetic cording is wrapped up in past conditioning and fear.

One of the greatest gifts of your new lifestyle will be the Divine guidance that directs you away from connections you created that no longer serve. If you've been in a relationship, whether a work, personal, or family relationship that you continually feel you're not benefiting by, go to quiet and access your intuitive knowing. Ask your higher self: Am I being served by this relationship on a higher level? Are the aspects of this relationship that I feel do not serve me in the physical world providing opportunities for me to transform aspects of my being that serve to make me a more conscious and loving person?

If you are shown areas where this relationship serves your growth, continue with it; if not, realize that this relationship has most likely run its course.

The wisdom of "Namaste and send them on their way" cannot be overemphasized. When we pause or end relationships, our conditioning is often triggered. Many of us don't know how to move on gracefully. Usually we need to make someone else wrong in order to feel right about leaving a relationship. But when you "Namaste and send a beloved of yours on their way," you are blessing the person you are leaving, knowing that they have their path, their gifts, and their challenges, and so do you. There is no need for recrimination, for anger, or for creating more pain. There is simply the acknowledgment that this relationship has served its purpose and that you are both free to move forward.

As each relationship has its own history, tenor, and form there is no one way for you to move forward. The only guidance you need is your personal connection with your highest wisdom and

- the awareness to notice whether a relationship is serving you,
- your willingness to check in with Source and inquire as to the higher-octave relevance of the relationship, if any, and
- the courage to move forward when needed.

CHUCK'S STORY
Moving Forward in Trust

Relationships are not the only major changes you will see during this stage of your development. Places where you live, homes that you love, and employment that you counted on might need to be changed, and your ability to go with the flow as you listen to your higher guidance will result in the peace that you will experience and the abundance that you're able to manifest. This has been the life-long experience of my longtime friend Chuck, who shares the story of how the process of trusting and letting go with love has always served his highest good.

Looking back over my life, I can see how trusting in my highest knowing to guide me as my life unfolded has led to the many opportunities and relationships that have become my history.

I trusted in Divine guidance early on, and as my life unfolded I received many opportunities to see how choosing my action from love created abundance and peace.

As a young man I had studied and learned gemology and jewelry making in New York, and after a heart-wrenching breakup with my girlfriend, who at the time I believed was the love of my life, I felt I needed a change.

While I was reeling from heartbreak, I intuitively knew I was supposed to be in California, so I listened to my higher knowing and took off cross-country in my old Ford van. This was a leap of faith as I had not a whole lot ahead of me except a couch to sleep on in Santa Cruz.

The journey took a month, and soon after I arrived I was presented an opportunity to study jewelry design with one of the best jewelers in the world: a seventy-five-year-old Frenchman who was, not surprisingly, also a yoga teacher, a strict vegan, and a true Renaissance man. He became my sensei.

After studying under my teacher and mentor I felt called to open my own shop. It immediately became very successful, and I had met the woman of my dreams, whom I married and have been married to for over thirty-eight years.

I brought a friend from New York out to become a partner in my business because I hoped to help him leave his drug addiction behind. It was my wish that teaching him a trade would turn his life around. But unfortunately that was not his path, and he got deeper into his addiction. It was an extremely difficult time because I felt torn between what I knew was best for my highest good and being there for my friend. After a few years of drama created by my friend's addiction and after much meditation, I decided to let my friend have the business I had created, leave everything, and go to Hawaii. Hawaii had always been a dream place to live for me, and I realized I once again needed to follow my highest calling.

I let all my clients, suppliers, and vendors know I was leaving, and when my wife and I arrived on Maui, I rented a car and drove straight to the top of Haleakala Crater at twelve thousand feet.

I wasn't prepared for the cold, but I stayed overnight in my car to watch the famous sunrise from the crater. I knew I was once again in the right place at the right time.

Feeling completely transformed and connected to a higher vibration, I then went to a small organic market and asked around looking for a contact I had been given, only to find that he was standing across from me.

My new friend provided a place for my wife and me to live, and I began to look for a new job. During my search, I ended up meeting a man who was one of the world's most recognized jadeite, pearl, and Oriental Art experts. While he told me there were no job openings with his organization at that time, he recommended me to another top jeweler across the street. I felt and knew in my highest knowing I was destined to work with this expert. After just a few weeks, he contacted me and said that his jeweler had suddenly left and asked if I wanted to work for him.

After working and studying with him for a year, I opened my own business again and became highly successful, servicing his store and seventy-five other retail jewelers on Maui and in Hawaii.

What I've learned through all the twists and turns in my life *is that out of darkness always comes the light. Trusting my higher self and letting go with love has always created something bigger, better, and more fulfilling. This same process has continued in my life leading to new careers and new options in every area of my life.*

At sixty-six years old, I am still in the process. And even when it seems difficult and I don't know where, how, or what is going to happen, I do know that if I focus on my why and stay connected to the higher power of who I am, it always is beautiful and fulfilling and serves my purpose as a human on this planet.

Reading through Chuck's words, you can sense his deep commitment to responding to life's twists and turns from a higher vibration of love. Love is a frequency that is open and allows for all possibilities, even those we cannot even begin to imagine.

Each time Chuck left behind that which no longer served his highest good and acted, whether it was to move across the country or from one mentor to another, he found another opportunity that moved him forward, not only in his physical life, but in his ability and willingness to be open to the idea that he did not need to know what was ahead.

This is what is called moving forward in trust, knowing that you are guided. Logic should not be your navigational tool; rather, allow your inner knowing to be your guide.

It is the Divine that opens you and enables you to take the leap in front of you.

Trust and faith are the tools that have sustained you during difficult transitions whether you knew they were there or not. Trust and faith work hand in hand and are powerful tools that are available for you to access at any time in your life. As they have always been there for you to draw upon in your earlier days before you were aware of their presence, you most likely experienced them sporadically.

Each time you walked in trust you built your capacity for faith. Early on in your life you may not have even consciously asked to be in trust, and yet as you look back, you see it was there. Before you even became aware that you could deliberately build your awareness you have already had opportunities to build your faith.

In the beginning days of your transformation you'll have the opportunity to consciously turn to trust, as Chuck did, when you are faced with life-defining decisions. This will be a new process for you and another opportunity to override your conditioning and make a choice that is for the highest good of who you are.

Often, choosing for your highest good will not be the most logical choice, and as you are conditioned to believe that your brain is the epicenter for all decision-making, it may be an effort for you to believe in the guidance you are being given. That's why the word *trust* is so appropriate. For not only are you believing and acting on information that did not come from your brain, but you're choosing to take a step without being able to see the bottom of the stairs.

As your life moves forward and you have experience after experience, where you have trusted and opened to receive Divine guidance and the results of your choices were so perfectly what you needed on all levels of your existence—not just on the level of physicality—your faith will indeed become a core frequency that is strengthened with every challenge you meet with trust by your side.

Continual trust builds your faith, and over time trust is no longer needed as your faith is solid and sustains you in every aspect of your life.

Following in Faith

I have always felt that faith is defined as holding the belief in something without needing evidence to say it is true. And then there is the beautiful definition of faith by Tagore: "Faith is the bird that feels the light when the dawn is still dark."

As universal as it is, faith is extremely personal.

We all see, feel, experience, and access our faith in different ways, and we choose to activate it at different times.

For me, faith is my deepest knowing. It is not something that I now need to choose or control, and I am grateful that I no longer visit faith and then leave it behind. Faith is now such a constant in my life that I'm certain that much of my peace comes simply from its unshakable presence.

But it hasn't always been that way.

It has been remarkable to witness my trust and then faith develop over the past thirty years. It seems that in my early days there was always a level of trust that was there, but I chose to recognize and access it only when challenging life events occurred. When I recognized myself in fear I would remind myself that I was blessed.

For me now, the knowledge of being blessed has come from a volume of direct experience. As I look back on my life I realize there are patterns and places in my life where I notice Spirit continually showing up. One place in particular has always been my home. Regardless of my financial state, I have always been guided to homes that were safe, beautiful havens.

There was the time when I was sixteen years old, I'd left home with seventy-five dollars in my pocket and no one at my back. I'd landed on a city block of rooming houses filled with cockroaches and drug addicts and was guided by Spirit to the one apartment house run by a lovely, kind old Italian woman.

My room was not only clean and sunny, but it contained a bed covered with a velvet and satin quilt and a lovely marble and granite fireplace.

Years later, when my husband and I were about to welcome our second son into the world, we lived in a small house that didn't have enough room for two children, and we were eager to move. But the housing market was not working in our favor: we had no savings at that point, and moving was not an option.

Then one day a few weeks after Sam was born, I went to the mailbox and found a check for $53,000 made out to me. I was stunned. I had no idea where it came from until I read the letter within. My mother had died suddenly six weeks before, and the check represented a portion of her retirement account. My mom had always been a hardworking, loving being who was never wealthy, so receiving this gift from her was completely unexpected.

We bought our new house the following month during a particularly difficult snowy winter in New England. There was over three feet of snow on the ground when we went to visit the house that would become our new home, and I carefully slid over the ice to the front door with Sam in a baby pack and Jake's little hand in mine to where the real estate agent was waiting to greet us.

Of all the questions I could have chosen, I felt compelled to ask her if there were any gardens on the property, but she had no knowledge of any.

Two months later, after our closing, I drove Jake and Sam up to the new house. It was a beautiful spring day, and Jake at three and a half years was finally old enough to play the forsythia game that my mother had played with my sister and brother and me when we were young. My mother always loved forsythia because they were the first blooms of spring. The game was really simple: as we were driving in the car the first person to see forsythia in bloom would shout out, "Forsythia!"

As we traveled to the house, we saw a few forsythia bushes, and as we turned onto our new street we saw a few more here and there. But when we arrived at our new house forsythia was in bloom everywhere! On a street that was three-quarters of a mile long, one that I would travel on for the next twenty years, our house was the only one completely decorated with hedges and bushes of forsythia in front, along the sides, and in the back of the property.

As the boys and I ended our initial visit and journeyed down the street on our way back to our current home, I looked at the name of the street as I realized I had never made note of it. As I read the sign, I gasped. The name of the street was Ethan Allen Drive. While the street was named after the patriot Ethan Allen, that name had a more personal meaning to me. My mother's favorite furniture store was Ethan Allen, and right before she died she finally had enough money to fill her house with the furniture she had always loved and coveted. I was completely excited with tears running down my face as I realized that my mother had not only provided the financial means, but directed me energetically to the home that she felt her grandchildren should be raised in. I stopped the car for a moment and thanked my mother for giving us the home that we all would treasure for the next twenty years.

In 2013, I sold the home we had bought when Sam was only three and a half months old and Jake was three and a half years. Sam was now twenty, and Jake was twenty-four. My brain injury occurred two days before closing on the sale of the house, and it's remarkable how I was left completely in the hands of Spirit. I opened fully and completely to the Divine with a depth of faith that I had never before experienced. Each move I was directed to take defied the logical choice for a woman with a brain injury who had no idea of when she would work again.

My faith led me to the six homes in the next seven years that Spirit directed me to. While moving continually was not anything I was eager to do, I never doubted the direction that came through. I followed in trust, and each home was exactly what I needed at the time. Remarkably, each spot was a beautiful, safe, warm, and aesthetically pleasing sanctuary, even though my finances would have landed me on a friend's couch if I chose logic as my guide. Each time that I was directed by Source to pack up to go to a new home, my friends were concerned and found it a bit unusual—but I never hesitated, knowing that I was guided by a higher authority.

Take a few moments now and discover if there are places where you have been continually blessed. As you look back, are there aspects of your life where it seems as if you have always been guided? Where have you seen guidance show up in relationships, romance, your financial situation, your health, or your career?

As you sit in contemplation and review your history, take note as to when you chose logic and when you trusted your intuition/guidance when decisions were at hand.

Perhaps you'll notice for the first time where and how the Divine has been actively present in your life. Commit here and now to not simply visiting with Divine guidance now and then, but choosing to open to its loving arms 24/7.

In your new lifestyle, you are ready to leave the old-paradigm belief that logic should be guiding your Lifestream, and you are ready to open to your new guidance system of trust and faith.

Let the gift of Divine guidance fill you to the brim. Sit in gratitude, filling every cell in your body with the divine light of love and appreciation not only for the presence of the Divine in your life but for your willingness to open up here and now, fully and completely.

As you make this proclamation and commit to being guided by your higher knowing, you open and prepare to continue creating the extraordinary life you have long sought.

While your work is far from over, Beloved, the adventure, the discoveries, and the appreciation for your new life as energy in form, guided by your highest knowing and actuated through the physicality of your body and brain, will be continually experienced.

No longer are you a physical body having an occasional mystical experience. You now know that you are seeded with high-vibrational energy that you can access at any time you choose. You believe in the depths of your being that there is a higher-octave reason for absolutely everything that occurs in your life, and you open to higher guidance to lead you to your decisions.

As difficulties occur you respond to each from an aspect of the high frequency of love that you experience every single day. You are excited as you awaken each day because your new lifestyle has taken hold, and you now walk your planet as an energetic being having a physical experience.

As you move forward with your new relationship to the Divine guiding you, you will continue to strengthen your core of faith as the challenges presented by the three-dimensional world continue, along with the many rewards!

10

What Your Extraordinary Life Will Deliver

Transformational Goal: *Living the Work*

Welcome home, Beloved!

At this part of your journey, you have released much of your conditioning and are consistently open to your Divine nature as the directional tool for your Lifestream 24/7. Day by day you are now beginning to walk in the physical world as the loving being that you truly are. I trust you've been noticing some of the many rewarding aspects of this work: the peace that comes from living in gratitude for what is, rather than wanting more; the freedom of releasing old stories and the pleasure of living in the present moment; the rewards of experiencing difficulties as gifts, replacing judgment with compassion, and receiving the gifts of synchronicity and miracles as the results of aligning your individual frequency with the universal field of love.

As you continue to keep your awareness in your front pocket, noticing when you're in low frequency and choosing to transform your state by using one of the many practices in this book, you will continue to increase your personal vibration. As your frequency rises, you will experience a deeper sense of gratitude, peace, and wholeness. You will be able to sustain longer periods of emotional neutrality and continue to heighten your newly increased awareness.

Your deep and continual connection with Source will manifest in different ways and provide opportunities for you to continue to see the many shifts and changes in your physical life that your efforts have produced.

I gently remind you that transformation is a very individual process. Each of us moves through the experience of letting go of societal and familial conditioning and opening to the Divine of who we are in different ways. There is no one timeline that each of us follows. That being said, as you progress and continue to have your highest knowing become your guidance system, you will begin to notice consistent, tangible, positive shifts in your responses to the places in your life that once caused you distress.

Situations that you had defined as difficult may no longer bother you. You may notice that qualities in lovers and partners and family members that you saw as irritating, you now find simply curious. This is a time when you begin to experience more patience and more compassion for yourself and others around you.

GRETCHEN'S STORY
From Judgment to Observation

My student Gretchen has been living this work for the past seven years. When we started our work together almost everything her husband did annoyed her. She always felt that she was working hard and rarely felt acknowledged or valued by him for who she was.

Soon after we began, Gretchen realized that each time her husband did something that she found irritating she would create and repeat stories about her husband and his lack of love and appreciation for her; she would tell these stories to herself and her friends over and over again. She was living inside of the vibration generated by the stories she created, and that painful energy was constantly charging her life and affecting her relationship with her husband long after each event was over.

As our work progressed and Gretchen began to replace the stories with the phrases discussed in chapter 7, "Wouldn't it be nice?" and "Isn't it curious?", she began to see a shift in how she felt about her husband. She was no longer fueling the previous hurts that she had experienced with repeated stories in the present, and as a result she began to *observe* her husband's and her own actions in a completely new light.

No longer in judgment and now in observation, she realized that even when she had felt incredibly tired and taxed, she would rarely ask her husband for help; but when she did, he was there for her. While he did not express his love and appreciation for her in ways she would've wished, when she observed his actions (rather than judging them through her expectations) she saw that he did express his love and gratitude for her; he simply didn't do it in the very specific ways that she would have liked. She realized that because she had *expectations* about how she wanted to be loved and appreciated, she had missed many of the efforts her husband had taken that expressed his own way of showing his love for her.

Interestingly, shortly after she had these aha moments and she actively began to let go of her judgments and expectations, she noticed that her husband became more open and receptive. She then made an effort to visualize his wonderful qualities daily, and she shared with him why she loved him and what she valued about him as a person. Without being consciously aware of it she was mirroring to him how she wanted to be loved. She was thrilled that eventually not only did he reciprocate in kind, but he suggested that they spend time together enjoying different activities that they hadn't shared in years.

~~~~~~~~~~~~~~~~~~~~~~~~~~~~

While we don't do our work to change how others perceive us, I have witnessed time and time again that how we walk in the world and the shifts we make to respond from love do truly affect us *all*. As we do our work, we get the opportunity to see how our local world responds.

How can they not, as we are all a part of the Oneness, the high frequency of love that we access over and over. While you may have the opportunity to see how your newfound consciousness affects those in your local world, you may never see how your efforts to become more loving have affected others in the world at large.

I assure you, my friend, that the work you do to lose your expectations and judgments is not only the greatest gift you can give yourself, but it is the most important effort you can contribute to our world.

As you continue creating your extraordinary life, you, too, will work more from observation than judgment, and in doing so you will become excited as you realize that your capacity for empathy and understanding has also greatly increased.

You may even feel called to become a beacon of light to others. While you may not be ready to shift your occupation and hang out a shingle promoting yourself as a spiritual guide, you will be filled with excitement and want others to have the sense of peace and equanimity that you now experience.

While it is a wonderful gift to share with others your newfound awareness, transformation, and peace, tread lightly and avoid the desire to proselytize or recruit. Instead, if you find yourself wanting to help those you love with your increased vibration and newly found perspective, consider using your higher frequency to provide healing.

As we are all energetic beings and we live within the energy of the field of Oneness, we hold within our Lifestream the capacity to heal ourselves and to provide restorative and beneficial frequency to others. As you live this work, you will bring healing to all.

Instead of your old practice of sharing your opinions, you can now participate in helping others to heal *vibrationally* from near and far. The practice below is a beautiful way to share the divine light with another in order to help heal them physically, mentally, or spiritually.

ACTION

✦

Cording Practice

This practice involves you entering into the energy field of another, often without their conscious knowing or permission. The only time we ever choose to enter another's energy field without their consent is when we are attempting to create a healing.

The practice below can be taken on to help an individual heal physically, mentally, emotionally, or spiritually; it will act as a deep and profound blessing and/or to heal your relationship with them.

To begin, make sure you have fifteen to twenty minutes of uninterrupted privacy and quiet.

+ Close your eyes and begin a pattern of breath through the nose by breathing long, full, deep, and easy inhale and exhale breaths.
+ Begin to relax the muscles in your body with every breath you take, keeping your attention fully on the rise and fall of the chest. Focus on making awareness of your breath your entire universe.
+ Once you feel totally relaxed and at ease, allow the visual of the being you are seeking to serve come into your consciousness. See them fully and completely, noting their physicality. Look them deeply in their eyes and feel them looking deeply into yours.
+ Then begin to sense your first chakra at the base of the spine open and visualize a cord being released. See or sense the cord of any thickness, any material, any color as it appears.
+ Watch as the cord leaves your chakra and immediately connects to the first chakra in the person you're seeking to heal.
+ Now bring your attention to each chakra in your body, from the first to the seventh one over the hairline, one at a time. As your attention is placed on each chakra as it opens, the cord within you is released, and it connects to the corresponding chakra of the person being healed.
+ Once all the chakras are opened and connected, begin to send the light of right action through the first chakra (at the base of the spine) from your body to the person being healed, making sure to place your full attention on the chakra being energized.

+ Now move on to the second chakra (in the area of the spleen) and be totally present as you pour the energy of love into the cord.
+ Then bring your attention to the third chakra (in the upper stomach), filling the cord with the energy of acceptance.
+ Move on to the fourth chakra (in the heart chamber) and amplify the light and beauty you see in the being by visualizing their many wonderful qualities.
+ Bring your attention to the fifth chakra (in the throat) and ask that they always speak and receive the truth in front of them through the energy of kindness.
+ Bring your attention to the sixth chakra (above the bridge of the nose between the brows of the eyes) and ask that they be connected to the light of their highest knowing.
+ When you come to the seventh chakra above the hairline, begin to visualize a ball of white, violet light.
+ See the white violet light move to the top of the center of their skull and then down through the top of their head and into their body. As the ball of light moves down, it overshadows the sixth chakra and releases the cord, which returns to your body. Then it sets the energy shared and seals that chakra.
+ Continue slowly as you see the white violet light move over the fifth, fourth, third, and second chakras, then down to the first chakra, always returning the cord to you, then setting the energy and sealing the chakra until the process is complete.
+ Stay in the energy of what was created until you feel called to come back into your body through the breath and then into the room.

The cording practice shared here is profound and powerful. Please, enter it with respect. Your intention must always be to assist your subject to walk in the highest good for themselves and for all.

If you are using this practice to heal the relationship between yourself and the person you are bringing in, make sure to keep your focus on sharing the many manifestations of love as directed above. You help to vibrationally heal the relationship between the two of you when you exchange high-frequency energy. It's the active sharing of Divine love that binds you together even more.

The energy of any words you hold as you share a frequency from chakra to chakra should not be around the two of you. Rather, the energy should be shared in order to increase the light within them. As you seek to fill them with light you, too, will be overshadowed by the field of the Oneness.

This practice should never be used to manipulate or create situations that fulfill your physical world desires. Please use it only to heal, support, or restore another being or your relationship with them. This is imperative.

I've had the opportunity for the last many years to listen to the stories my students shared as they used the practices suggested during our teachings. My student Monique used the cording process after our second teaching. She sought to build a closer relationship with her beloved teenage daughter, who was going through the process of separating from her mother, as many teenagers do. It was extremely painful for Monique; she wanted to provide guidance and support for her child, and she hoped to build closeness from afar.

She loved my explanation of the cording practice and thought it would be helpful with her daughter. Within hours of completing the practice of cording with her daughter energetically, they had a breakthrough. Her teen, not knowing anything about the energetic cording that had been done between them, asked to have a conversation with Monique, and during their talk opened up completely about her fears and concerns and her wishes for her life. Monique was totally ecstatic, as this was the first talk they'd had in quite some time.

While of course we never know why things occur, Monique has continued to use this cording practice with her daughter each time she feels the distance between them is too deep. Her child always responds within a day or so by reaching out for a conversation.

At this part of your journey you will be able to not only begin to help and heal others, but you may feel that your path is taking a turn and that becoming a coach, mentor, or spiritual teacher is your calling.

My student Simone was introduced to me when I was healing from my brain injury in New York City. She was a talented hairstylist at a high-end New York salon, and knowing of my financial predicament, she generously offered to provide me with her services at a discounted rate. Knowing that my physical impairment was an opportunity for me to practice being in full receivership, I gratefully accepted her kind offer.

Each time I sat in Simone's chair, Spirit came through me, and we had the most amazing conversations. Over time she attended teachings at my home, and then she became a one-on-one student. Simone had long had an interest in self-improvement, but the kind of spiritual teachings I provided were new for her. Shortly after our teachings began in earnest she became more actively involved in yoga, and a few years later she became a yoga instructor and a spiritual teacher. I have been delighted to watch her spiritual development unfold and to see her path expand as she takes her brilliance out into the world!

Finding Peace in the Present

Whether or not your journey takes you in the direction of healing or teaching, as you continue to grow I trust you will become more present to the many places in your life where you experience gratitude. You will notice that you no longer focus on what you don't have. Your old conditioned response of always wanting more will fade and disappear over time. This particular long-term habit was one of the last to leave for me.

When I was a little girl I remember so clearly wanting to be a teenager. When I was a teenager, I desperately wanted to leave home. When I left home, I wanted a romantic relationship. When I had a romantic relationship, I couldn't wait till it was over. When I had my next relationship, I couldn't wait to get married. When I got married, eventually I couldn't wait to get divorced. And on and on and on. Wherever I was, I wanted something different, something more than I had. All the while it was clear that my attention was not on what I was grateful for; it was on what I felt was my next station in life.

Always wanting more is a clear indication of living in the low frequency of lack. Does any of this sound familiar to you?

At this stage of your development if you've been reading the material and actively using the practices provided, you have most definitely begun to sense the patterns that you hold that do not serve. Perhaps you, too, are always wanting more? Or possibly your pattern looks very different. It truly matters not how your discomfort manifests. What is important is that you continue to place your attention on that which you choose to create more of.

If you still find yourself jealous of others, place your attention on becoming more generous. If you notice that you're impatient, practice tolerance and patience. Your work is to continue to notice where difficulty arises and then to place your attention on the high-frequency energy that directly corresponds to the low frequency you continually find yourself accessing.

At this stage this is a critically important ongoing process, for as you become conscious of difficulty and consistently replace it with higher frequencies, you will begin to experience sustained equanimity.

I have spoken so many times throughout this book about our attention and where we place it. For *we are our attention, and where we place our attention grows.*

In my early days while I was "growing" my consciousness, my attention was still always on what I felt I lacked. But as I grew my awareness and placed my attention consistently on the aspects of my life that I was grateful for, I found myself in a new state. I felt more present.

Ultimately, with gratitude as my constant companion, the desire to want something different no longer showed up. Initially it began to disappear during the infrequent times when I truly felt grounded in the present moment. As gratitude became a constant state and being in the moment became more and more my life practice, I noticed that I stopped wishing for life to be any different than it was, even when difficulty reared its head.

When you continually live in gratitude, the present moment becomes your normal state, and there can be no desire for anything else, because nothing else exists. That is the beauty of living in the present moment. There is literally nothing else.

That's when peace begins to truly settle in.

You may be right around the corner or quite a ways from this holy place, and while you have done much work and are well on your way to creating your exceptional life, it will serve you well to begin to understand the difference between expectations and wishes, observation and judgment.

When You Wish . . .

In chapter 4 I shared with you how your expectations of yourself, of others, and of situations are a part of your old paradigm. At this stage of your evolution, as expectations appear they do so to make you aware they need your attention in order to be released.

If you have already taken on the practice of observing and releasing your expectations as they appear, you are now ready for the graduate course: focusing your attention on wishes rather than expectations. This is an important key to manifesting that which you desire.

As with most of our work the difference between placing your attention on a wish or desire rather than an expectation is not subtle; it is actually a deep and profound shift.

An expectation is a manifestation of the egoic body and structured by the brain. It's low-frequency energy that you'll be able to recognize because it feels closed, like a demand. Expectations often come with specific parameters (often with deadlines) and can appear in relation to others or to yourself.

Remember my student Gretchen? She had very specific expectations around what it looked like to be loved by her husband. As he loved differently than she expected, she was unable to recognize his actions as supportive until she became aware that she was holding expectations that clouded her vision. Once she was able to lose her judgment of her husband's actions and placed herself in observation, she was able to notice the different steps he took that represented his love for her.

Expectations and judgments are different actions, yet often intertwined because they are both expressions of low-frequency energy. An expectation is the opposite of a wish. It is set and fixed. It carries a specific form in which you require it to appear and a certain time frame that you insist it to be met. With all of these strident, low-frequency rules, there is absolutely no room for the Divine to slip in and contribute.

I'm suggesting you replace your expectations with wishes, or desires, and please do replace judging others—and yourself—with the states of observation and grace.

At this point in your journey you will be able to hold wishes or desires instead of expectations. As you have already been practicing shifting your state in other areas, applying your attention to wishes when you notice yourself in expectation will be an easy change.

Wishes are alive; they are of light and have no deadlines. They come from your high energetic state of love, which is why they feel so alive and exciting.

In its nature a wish is open-ended and has no timeline. A wish holds the energy of magic within its core. It doesn't require any specific shape or form; it's spacious, allowing room for the Divine to complete the mission.

Remember this line in the song "When You Wish Upon a Star" you heard as a child?

> *If your heart is in your dream*
> *No request is too extreme*

Now *there's* a sign of the Divine!

As I've spoken of several times in previous chapters, when ideas, connections, or actions simply land in your awareness, with no prior thought on your part, the Divine is at work, and your wishes are the playground for the high frequency within you. The Divine wants nothing more than to deliver to you that which is for your highest good!

Observation is the tool that enables you to see what is truly present, noting the facts without an opinion attached. Are you putting forth wishes, or are you still in expectation? The tool of observation enables you to answer that question without a viewpoint added.

Judgment is your opinion of what you are observing.

Take a moment and think back.

Remember a recent time when you were in judgment of yourself. Did you scold yourself when you didn't complete a task? Did you berate yourself when you chose to eat something not on your new meal plan? Did you chide yourself when you lost your patience? In each of these cases you had set an expectation that you had wanted to meet, but were not in that moment able to meet, and then the seemingly automatic response of judgment set in. Judgment, like other low-frequency manifestations, is a distraction. It moves you further from the action you were hoping to take. As soon as you begin to judge, you're placing your attention on that which you did *not* want to create. As you place your attention on what you don't want, you are actually once again creating more of what you were hoping to lose.

As you move through the physical world, it will be important to replace your expectations with wishes or desires, and it's most helpful to use the high-vibrational tool of observation in order to see how you are moving toward that which you wish for. As always, what matters is the vibration that we move forward in.

As you *observe* your progress rather than judge it, you're already in an open state. If, in that open state, you witness that you didn't keep your commitment to yourself, note that and then stay in high frequency by giving yourself grace.

Grace is the ultimate high-frequency action. It is the equivalent of a holy pass. When you recognize that you wanted to try to shift a pattern but did not manage to do so, acknowledge what you *observed* and then lay that moment down. It's ok. You will try again.

That is grace.

As you are a vibrational being who seeks peace and equanimity, it is important at this level of your work that you to create as much positive vibration as possible.

If you're trying to make changes in how you walk in the world, and you create negative energy by judging yourself harshly each time you're unable to immediately elicit a change, you are working against your own process and not helping our collective.

Grace is a blessing that you can bestow upon yourself each time you need more time, more practice, and more love, because it leaves behind tons of positive vibrations and the distraction of guilt has no place to land.

Giving yourself grace is an act that comes more easefully as you learn how to shift from being mind- and brain-directed to living with faith and trust as your guiding lights.

Opening to Divine Direction

While I've been on a spiritual path for many years and I continually use all of the practices that I have shared with you, it was faith and trust that I relied on the most throughout the first five years of healing my brain injury.

I've shared with you that from the moment my car was hit, Spirit had come into the car and told me that I was protected (but the days ahead would not be easy), and I was told to completely surrender to whatever happened. You can't surrender and stay brain-centered, as logic has nothing to do with Divine guidance. I complied, and I gave up logic as my guide; since that moment faith and trust have been my guiding lights.

As the years progressed and I continued to be unable to work in a way that supported me, I trusted. I lived off my savings, and when that was gone, with my faith still strong, I watched as Spirit moved me from one location to another and created amazing opportunities that enabled me to continue to live a comfortable life, even though I was earning less and less each year.

There were many experiences that were divinely given to me that had me shaking my head in wonder and placing me in constant gratitude. What others would call synchronicities and miracles were everyday events that became constant companions to me.

You won't need a car event that takes you out of your life in order to experience the Divine as an active partner. At this point in your journey, continuing to do your work will enable you to witness the participation of the Divine within you. It is always active in your life, waiting for your awareness to recognize and activate its presence.

The Divine is *always* in attendance in our lives, yet we are only able to experience its existence when we have raised our vibration high enough to recognize and welcome it in.

As you've read this book, you have been increasing your personal vibration, and as you continue the practice of bringing your attention to the actions in your life that don't serve and replacing them with higher vibrational responses, you have prepared your Lifestream for your next important shift. It's now time to open to Divine direction!

Divine Direction is the act of moving forward in your life when Spirit directs you to. Once direction is received you then apply your excellent brain to work out the details.

This is likely quite different from your current, conditioned way of planning your life, for most of us have been taught to "think ahead" and "plan for the future."

Being divinely led is a 360-degree full circle departure from your conditioned training as it asks you to keep your intuitive body alert in order to hear guidance. Your marvelous thinking brain can then work out the plans that Spirit delivers, while you invoke faith and trust as your guides.

All these years, you have been trained to manipulate and to think your way out of situations. But your new way of life—trusting in the Divine to lead the way—is not about using your brain or wiles. This effort relies on your skills of observation and on your willingness to reflect, *and* it asks for your readiness to wait and be guided to a response.

As you are just now becoming comfortable with the idea of the Divine living within you, the lower frequency of the old patterns you may hold are still alive and active, which is why the tools of trust and faith will be so helpful.

As you continue to take on the practice of trusting and holding faith while being guided and then moving forward only when divinely directed to do so, you are leaving your egoic nature behind and invoking your intuitive body, which over time builds a core of neutrality within your Lifestream.

As the core builds and your personal frequency increases, you will begin to notice more and more experiences that you recognize as clear signs of Divine intervention.

Each experience of holy direction looks completely different. For me during my entire healing process, the Divine showed up continually in regard to where I lived and how my money arrived. During this time I was directed by Spirit to move six times in seven years.

Each time I was directed to move I wasn't thinking about moving at all, and the direction was always clear. It never appeared as an intellectual thought; it always felt as if Spirit just quietly landed a message inside my being.

And then there was the time when Spirit spoke quite loudly.

I was living in New York City (in my second apartment in two years) and having my hair styled at the salon where my student Simone worked her magic. Another stylist, a stranger to me, felt the need to share many details of her spiritual development. She started a long monologue telling me the story of her spiritual awakening, which began at an inn in Woodstock, New York, and took place over many years.

After she completed her ongoing story she looked straight into my eyes and said to me, "You need to go there." I knew in that moment that Spirit was speaking to me through this woman.

I immediately booked a room at the very inn she had spoken of. As I got off the bus two months later in the middle of town, Spirit told me that Woodstock would be my new home.

By now I knew that Spirit's message was an announcement and that the details would show up as needed, so I chose to keep this information in my front pocket, and I moved through my visit not focusing at all on Spirit's message. Many magical experiences occurred in my two-day visit, and something about the inn itself kept feeling like home.

The inn was situated on the Saw Kill River and it had two hammocks for guests, one on the river side and one by the garbage area. Obviously I wanted to sit in the hammock by the river, but Spirit kept loudly telling me to take the hammock by the garbage. I found this to be curious, but as I was comfortable following guidance, I rocked in the hammock by the garbage. In order to avoid looking straight at the trash, I found myself looking up through the woods to two houses that were perched high at the top of the hill.

As I walked around town I met many people, all of whom were kind, friendly, and welcoming. If this were to be my new home, Spirit had picked a wonderful spot. As I traveled back to New York City I met a woman on the bus and gave her a healing, and she in turn sent me links to the local paper so I could take a look at housing.

While I had just renewed my lease in New York City, I still went online to look for rentals in Woodstock. I was just going to take a look. There was only one house listed, and it sounded marvelous, but it was a bit over my budget. However, Spirit said to call.

I spoke to the landlord on the phone and found out that he owned the inn where I had stayed and that the house for rent was way at the top of the property above the garbage area. It was one of the houses that I kept being drawn to look at when I was swinging in the hammock by the trash!

I met the landlord a few days later in Woodstock, and when he asked me why I wanted to move to town I told him the story of being spiritually directed to his inn. He bent over backward to help make renting his beautiful home financially feasible for me.

Living guided by the Divine is a very different life than living from logic. If I was living in the world directed by my brain, I would not have gone to Woodstock. It was never on my radar, and money was rarely available for weekend trips. I would have listened to the story being shared with me and would have been grateful that Spirit sent my storyteller to me so I could witness for her. I would not have had Spirit yelling in my ear to GO!

But I am a woman directed by the Divine.

When the stylist spoke to me directly, *I knew* I was to go to Woodstock for a visit. When I got off the bus and heard Spirit telling me this was my new home, *I knew* I was to wait for further direction. When I saw the home advertised in the paper and logically knew that it was more than I could afford, and Spirit told me to call anyway, I called. When the landlord of the house told me he owned the inn that I had been directed to stay in and that the house that I was calling about was one of the houses that Spirit had continually guided my sight to while I was on the hammock, *I knew* I was to live in that house. And then when the landlord asked me why I wanted to move to Woodstock, *I knew* I was to be honest and tell him the truth that I had been directed there by Source.

I had done nothing but leave my logic behind, follow Spirit's direction, and share my truth with my landlord.

Spirit took care of the details.

When I moved to Woodstock, I felt as if I had landed in heaven. I was given a beautiful house on the Saw Kill River surrounded by forests, bear, and deer. I spent most of my time alone there writing this book. I developed a few friendships along the way, and one of the people I met in Woodstock was Nancy, who became not only my friend but the editor of this book! I was in Woodstock for one and a half years during which time I discovered that my landlord, Tom, was the husband of one of my very favorite authors, Elizabeth Lesser, who cofounded the Omega Institute, one of the first spiritual retreat centers in the country.

Clearly Spirit brought me to the home I was meant to be in as I continued to heal and write this book.

My work was not over, and within eighteen months of living in the house, I was given my greatest opportunity to date to once again practice faith and trust. This time, however, it wasn't glorious or fun; it was truly difficult and challenging. With my brain almost fully healed, I struggled for the first time in years to hold my center of faith and trust.

It was October of my second year in Woodstock, and my income began to dry up considerably. I had taken on a larger overhead with the house and was concerned because I had no savings. I asked Spirit for direction. I heard: "Stay where you are, be in trust and faith until we give you direction to move." I followed their advice and for the next five months my income continually dwindled. By January I was barely able to pay my bills, yet Spirit continued to tell me to wait.

For the first time in years and with my brain well on the way to complete healing, it became hard for me to hold my faith. In February, I pleaded with Spirit to please, *please* provide me direction. Admittedly, I was starting to feel desperate. I had never asked for guidance this way before. In fact, it had been years before my brain injury since I had felt any lack of faith.

Spirit's answer at that point was for me to sell everything I had that wasn't important to me and to store everything else. I was stunned. Spirit told me that I wouldn't have a constant place to live for the next year. I was also advised to wait for a forthcoming invitation.

This was clearly not the advice I was hoping for.

In my fear I bypassed the words about an invitation and went directly to the idea of being homeless. As I had left home at age sixteen to create my own space in the world, the idea of home had been always extremely important to me. After living in Massachusetts for forty years and in my house for twenty, I had recently moved three times in four years, and each spot became my home in its own unique way.

In the past five years, all of my plans for my future disappeared, I lost my income, and I didn't know when, or if, I would ever heal, yet during that time I was easily able to follow Spirit's direction, and I had always been given a home, but now the idea of being homeless scared me to death.

I consciously noted the fear that gripped me and knew I needed to move beyond it. I wasn't quite ready to do so, but I placed myself in grace and reminded myself that Spirit had plans that I couldn't see and that my job was to use the fear in order to move myself forward.

I chose to use my well-worn practices, the very ones I've shared here with you, and I followed Spirit's guidance to sell my belongings.

Even though I loved the house and everything about living in Woodstock, I knew it had been a gift to me and now I was to once again follow Spirit's guidance to leave. It felt important to treat each step of moving out of the house as a celebration. I organized a massive yard sale and invited my beloved cousin Carol and her husband Dave to join me.

We had a wonderful time setting up for the sale, and on the day of the event there was a continual line out the door. We met many new neighbors, had lovely, meaningful conversations, and I sold two-thirds of my possessions.

After the sale, sitting inside of a nearly empty house, not knowing where I was to go or what I was to do, I spent many days in gratitude for the time I had in the Hudson Valley and spent much time in prayer and meditation, awaiting direction.

While I waited I felt directed to call my beloved spiritual teacher, Hope. I asked if I could visit her center for a few days to clear my energy field. I didn't share what was going on; I just asked to visit for a brief time. She laughed and said that she felt called to invite me to stay for six months instead of a few days, and would I accept her invitation to be a teacher in residence at her spiritual center?

Here was the invitation that Spirit had mentioned, the very one that I had forgotten! To be given such a beautiful invitation, to live inside my teacher's spiritual home and be able to contribute to the community while I wrote this book, was a supreme gift. Being a teacher in residence was the reason that I wouldn't have needed my own home for the next year.

What had happened to me in the years since my car event but before Hope's invitation had arrived?

I had been living a life where I had absolutely no physical world security, but due to my ongoing work to use difficulty as a tool to go to peace, I had remained open to Divine direction regardless of what was happening. And it served me well.

Spirit had brought me to home after home, each one perfectly suited for what I needed at the time. Finally, I was brought to Woodstock, which provided me the home I needed in the country surrounded by nature, where I was introduced to the editor for this book.

When my time and purpose in Woodstock was nearing the end, another exciting purposeful episode was about to begin, but I had no knowledge of that. When my money dried up with no revenue stream in sight, with a healthy brain that for the first time in five years began to work overtime, I embraced fear for the first time in a really long time.

Yet the Divine within me had already reached a tipping point, and even when I felt lost, I wasn't. The Divine was still at work.

While in fear I still used my practices of going to quiet, to prayer, to meditation—and they helped me to observe my state with radical honesty and constantly shift back to a neutral spot. I recognized that it was my ego and newly healthy brain that created the fear that caused the discomfort I experienced. As I continually shifted from worry and fear to faith and trust, over and over and over again, I was continually returning to a high vibration. Even though fear was present, it was never constant due to my practices.

Many people hearing this story would say the Universe was testing me. But you and I both know this was no test.

It was an opportunity to repeatedly practice returning to a high vibration of love—even though my conditioning and sense of financial responsibility told me to move and I was increasingly uncomfortable. Instead of following the fear, I observed my state. I listened to Spirit, and I continued to shift from fear to love over and over.

When Hope's invitation arrived, I understood that my ego had created the worry and doubt I had experienced.

FALSE EVIDENCE APPEARING REAL had never had more meaning for me. Nothing had actually happened in the past five months to create my fear. I had never missed a rent payment or utility bill. My previous conditioning and my healthy brain completely invented the concern.

Within a short period of time I had packed and stored what little I had left of my belongings, and I moved to the Hope Interfaith Center in Mankato, Minnesota, where I had a glorious six months finishing the writing of this book and sharing teachings with the community while living at HIC.

When my six months at HIC ended I was directed by Spirit to return to Boston because I would be needed by my family. I had hoped to return to Woodstock, but as always, I followed direction and landed back in Massachusetts at an opportune time to support my eldest son and his wife.

I share this story with you, Beloved, as it is such a beautiful example of how the Divine is always working in our lives, even when we lose our way. It speaks to how difficulty can indeed be purposeful when we choose to use it for the development of our consciousness. And finally, it tells us all that we are never too evolved to be asked to deepen, to further our commitment to the work that we have taken on.

We are always being guided, even when we feel lost. I've learned that my not being able to hold faith and trust was in itself an opportunity for me to move forward in honesty and to open *even more fully* to receivership.

My honesty with my teacher about how I felt lost and needed support and my request to visit the center for a few days was me moving forward in radical honesty and asking to receive.

The honesty piece had not been difficult for me for years, but asking to receive? That had been my continual lesson!

The work for us—for you and for me—will always continue. Regardless of whether we are able to completely move forward in trust and love, the Divine will always be within us, and the opportunities to return home to the high frequency of love—who we are as our continual state—never leaves.

But we have come to the end of this part of our journey together. I trust that the teachings, the wisdom, and the practices that Spirit has shared through me will be honored, valued, and utilized by you, time and time again.

For in your hands, Beloved, you are holding the guide book that will lead you into a world where you—high-frequency energy in physical form—can truly live your extraordinary life to the fullest.

For that is certainly what you so rightly deserve!

Index